To Dr. David Beckman—
professor, encourager, and friend—
for your life of faithfulness and commitment
to our Lord Jesus Christ
as president and chancellor of Colorado Christian
University.

———

© 1995 by Gary L. McIntosh
All rights reserved
Printed in the United States of America

Published by:
Broadman & Holman Publishers
Nashville, Tennessee

Designed by: Steven Boyd

4261-87
0-8054-6187-6

Dewey Decimal Classification: 250
Subject Heading: Church Work \ Christian Ministry \ Lay Ministry
Library of Congress Card Catalog Number: 95-6528

Library of Congress Cataloging-in-Publication Data
McIntosh, Gary L.
The exodus principle : a 5-part strategy to free your people for ministry /
Gary L. McIntosh
        p. cm.
Includes bibliographical references (p.)
ISBN 0-8054-6187-6 (HB)
1. Lay Ministry. 2.Church leadership. 3. Church Growth. I. Title.
    BV677.M35   1995
    253.x—dc20
    95-6528   CIP
    99 98 97 96 95 5 4 3 2 1

Contents

Empower Your People

One of my friends was pastoring a church that had grown dramatically during his first three years of ministry. He was an excellent strategist who effectively led his church to develop a plan for church growth, rallied church members behind it, and executed the plan flawlessly. After plotting the church's first three years of numerical growth on a graph, he then projected the next five years of growth. From most viewpoints it appeared the church would become one of the largest in his city within a few years.

The church was a model of a well-planned and executed ministry. Technically all was in place for continued growth. By the fourth year, however, attendance had fallen significantly and it never reached the projections of growth that earlier had seemed so certain. The reason? That church failed to reach its potential because the people involved did not realize that the heart of a healthy church is service.

The members' unwillingness to serve first became prominent in the child care ministry. Attendance at the traditional evening worship service had been declining, so the church leaders started a new Sunday evening Bible institute modeled after a local community college's evening adult classes. This new approach to Sunday evening ministry worked well for about six months until problems arose with child care. As it turned out, no one was willing to watch the children on Sunday evening while other adults were involved in the classes. Several options for providing child care were tried, such as hiring people from outside the church, rotating child care among church members on a quarterly time schedule, and requiring church leaders to take a turn caring for children in the nursery. Yet every option was blocked. No matter what approach was attempted, people were just unwilling to serve in this crucial area of ministry.

After nearly six months of frustrated efforts, the church board called a meeting of all parents and interested individuals to develop a plan for Sunday evening child care. This meeting ended with a decision to provide no child care for the Sunday evening Bible classes. With no child care available, families with children stopped attending and eventually the entire Sunday evening ministry was cancelled due to poor attendance. Unfortunately, the lack of willingness to serve in the Sunday evening child care ministry was an indication of an even greater unwillingness to serve in other areas of ministry. Even though many mechanical aspects for growth were in place—plans, strategies, goals—the church suffered decline due to the people's unwillingness to serve one another.

Serving One Another Sacrificially

There are few who would argue that churches are to be characterized by loving and sacrificial service. Christ made this evident when His disciples James and John and their mother approached Him asking to sit on His right and left side in His kingdom. His answer set the tone of true ministry: "You know that the rulers of the Gentiles lord it over them, and their great men exercise authority over them. It is not so among you, but whoever wishes to become great among you shall be your servant, and whoever wishes to be first among you shall be your slave; just as the Son of Man did not come to be served, but to serve, and to give His life a ransom for many" (Matt. 20:25–28).

My friend's church was not characterized by such sacrificial service. People literally lorded it over each other by insisting on being served while exhibiting little willingness to serve others. The child care issue was just evidence of a more basic problem. A lack of sacrificial service to others eventually undermined an otherwise fine church with outstanding potential for growth.

I share this story with you because I think it is important to stress that the core of church growth is spiritual, not technical. All experience shows that even a superbly organized and planned ministry will eventually fail without the active care, love, and service of people toward others. The finest strategies and plans for church growth will have limited effect if a spirit of service is not found in our churches. Although this seems obvious, many churches appear to believe they can use all the church growth techniques available without improving the attitudes, atmosphere, and actions of their congregations.

People who need Christ will be drawn to our Lord as they see us loving each other (see John 13:34–35), not because our techniques are sound. Yes, we need to be sure the strategic side of our ministry is solidly in place. People will be turned away from our Lord if we conduct ministry in a sloppy and thoughtless manner. The underlying reason people are drawn to Christ is our loving service for each other. Remember: Christ did not say all people will know that we are His disciples if we have a mechanically sound ministry. Rather, He said they will know we are His disciples if we have love for one another.

God is in charge of the local church. Despite our hard work, God's strength empowers church programs and ministries. Prayer is our only way to tap into this infinite supply of strength. Neglect prayer and we neglect the health and vitality of our churches.

In our computerized culture, we tend to substitute technique (systems and procedures, committees, job descriptions, budgeting, and staff retreats) for prayer. Human power is no match for God's power.

We don't have all the answers to church strategy—where our church should be headed, what programs will work best, or how to empower lay leaders. We need humility to admit that our vision is myopic at times and that we grope our way along more often than we care to admit.

We must recognize our limitations and lean on God's guidance. We're like a sailboat pilot who knows that, although he or she steers the craft, the mighty wind powers it across the water.

—Philip Van Auken, "Five Mission Ingredients," *Growing Churches*, April/May/June 1993, 57.

Love is demonstrated as we serve each other. The apostle Paul pointed out that our freedom in Christ should not be used as "an opportunity for the flesh, but through love serve one another" (Gal. 5:3–15). While the "MEism" of past decades is slowly turning into "WEism" in this decade, many of our churches appear to be comprised of people who are using their freedom in Christ for personal pleasure (opportunity for the flesh) rather than for sacrificial service to others—either inside or outside their church. I believe that many churches face a similar problem as my friend's church in that their plans for growth fail because their strategies are technical, intellectual, and sterile; they do not appeal to the heart of the issue—sacrificial service.

Empowering a Spirit of Service

In the past few years empowerment has gained recognition in the business community. This concept is not new to our communities of faith. God empowered His people from the very beginning of the church to minister to the world. Christ's final words to His disciples declared, "but you shall receive power when the Holy Spirit has come upon you; and you shall be My witnesses both in Jerusalem, and in all Judea and Samaria, and even to the remotest part of the earth" (Acts 1:8). After the Holy Spirit came on the Day of Pentecost (Acts 2), His indwelling power allowed the early disciples to effectively serve their world and each other (see Acts 2:41–47).

We also are an empowered people. The same Holy Spirit who empowered the early disciples for service empowers us to serve each other and our world today. The idea of empowerment goes beyond the simple truth of the availability of power, however. Empowerment is an active term. It has reference to the giving of authority and responsibility from one in charge to a subordinate.

In a business, empowerment takes place when a manager delegates part of his or her responsibility for making decisions to subordinates and then actually allows the subordinates to exercise the authority. Empowerment in the church takes place when pastors and church leaders delegate responsibility for ministry to their people and actually allow them to execute it. Empowering people in our churches means that pastors and church leaders allow those who are followers to participate or act on the power that they already have through the Holy Spirit.

Empowering the people is precisely what church leadership is all about. As leaders, our role is not to control those under us but to empower them by granting to them permission to become engaged in ministry. Speaking of gifted leaders, the apostle Paul wrote, "And He gave some as apostles, and some as prophets, and some as evangelists, and some as pastors and teachers, for the equipping of the saints for the work of service, to the building up of the body of Christ" (Eph.4:11–12).

If Paul were writing to believers today he might have written, "for the *empowering* of the saints for the work of service." While the words *equipping* and *empowering* have their different meanings, the ultimate idea is the same. Paul tells us that the prime reason leaders exist in our churches is to give away ministry, not control ministry.

Of course, this godly leadership is difficult. Pastors and church leaders have to give up control and place their trust in those whom they may have little confidence. From the church members' point of view, receiving empowerment for ministry is also a little fearful because they are given more responsibility for ministry than they have ever had before and they may stumble in their attempt to exercise it. Yet we will never advance the kingdom of God like we have been commanded to do without empowered people. Consequently, we cannot empower people to serve unless both parties are willing to take the risks involved.

It has been humbling for me to look back at churches I have pastored and observe what ministries or programs have lasted or ceased to exist since I left. I became the pastor of one church in 1976. It was a small church of fifty-four people that had almost closed its doors. In my youthful exuberance, I hit the ground running and started a children's program, Tuesday evening visitation, direct mail advertising, a Thanksgiving Harvest Dinner, and other similar types of programs. Later, one of our members suggested that we begin a preschool targeted to unchurched families and single parents in our community. The church board empowered him to move ahead on the project. He organized a team of interested members, did all the research, raised the money, and shared the vision with the church body. The preschool was in place within a few months and became the most successful outreach ministry the church had ever started. About the same time, I suggested we begin a small group program, but instead of my leading it, our board empowered some interested members to take responsibility for designing and executing the ministry. I attended a small group but never led one. The people did almost all of the work of ministry themselves.

I left that pastorate twelve years ago, but I've kept in contact with many of the people and find it insightful to hear their reflections of my time with them. Every ministry I started there was dropped soon after I left—the children's ministry, the direct mail outreach, the Harvest Dinner, and the Tuesday evening visitation. Yet the preschool remains a vital aspect of the church's ministry to the community. Further, in a recent conversation with a few of the members, I learned that their main remembrance of my years of ministry with them were the small groups. The ministries that continue are not the ones I started but the ones that church members were empowered to research, develop, and execute on their own.

After hundreds of years in captivity, God sent Moses and his brother Aaron to Pharaoh with a simple message: "Let My people go that they may celebrate a feast to Me in the wilderness" (Exod. 5:1). God's people were in bondage and not free to serve their Lord. They needed to be empowered, or given freedom, to exercise their God-given calling of worship. After much struggle, they eventually were released from Egypt but found themselves caught in a different kind of bondage. Moses quite naturally felt he had to do everything. He was the one who was trained and knew the statutes and laws of God. Thus, he judged the people from morning to night, wearing himself out and frustrating the people who could not get their disputes resolved. It took Jethro, his father-in-law, to point out the obvious: "The task is too heavy for you; you cannot do it alone" (Exod. 18:18).

People in our churches often find themselves in a similar situation. They have been called out of the bondage of sin and empowered by the Holy Spirit for ministry. Yet when they attempt to become involved in ministry, they find they are in bondage to a church culture and system that prevents them from doing so.

As church leaders, we need to hear Jethro's words to Moses and God's words to Pharaoh over and over again; "Let My people go." "You cannot do it alone." The goal of our church should be to empower every member and regular attender to serve others by taking ownership of the ministry and having the freedom to exercise their God-given calling. *The Exodus Principle* is intended to assist you as a pastor or church leader to begin empowering your community of believers to superior service.

A Preview of Things to Come

The Exodus Principle is intended to be a reference manual that may be consulted again and again on how to empower your community of believers to superior service!

In part 1, "Designing a Culture of Service," you will uncover

- ways to develop a new culture of service in your church which will result in a new level of pride and care;
- practical ideas for putting people first in your ministries;
- steps for involving people in personal ministry so that they grow in their commitment to serving others.

———

In part 2, "Preparing for a Culture of Service," you will discover

* how to use "Moments of Truth" to create positive impressions about your church in the minds of guests;
* ways to assist members to identify with the "Pride Factor" and become experts in "guest relations";
* procedures for improving core church ministries.

———

In part 3, "Communicating a Culture of Service," you will learn

* how to develop good word-of-mouth rumors about your church;
* ways to say hello to your community to increase name recognition and attract more guests;
* steps for starting new ministries which will touch the hearts of guests and attract them to Christ.

———

In part 4, "Practicing a Culture of Service," you will determine

* ways to greet guests during their first visit to your church.
* how to welcome guests without offending them;
* approaches to following up guests that are appropriate to your culture and yet provide a measure of extra value.

———

In part 5, "Empowering a Culture of Service," you will construct

* pathways of belonging to assist guests in becoming involved in the life of your church;
* insights for empowering a culture of service in the life of your church.

———

Empowering People—A Summary

♦ Our churches are to be characterized by sacrificial service. Christ set the example for ministry in Matthew 20:20–28 where He reminds us that "the Son of Man did not come to be served, but to serve, and to give His life a ransom for many" (v. 28).

♦ The core of church growth is spiritual, not technical. Even if the technical aspects of ministry are in place—plans, strategies, goals—a church will probably not grow unless members exhibit a spirit of service to one another and to those people the church is trying to reach.

♦ People who need Christ will be drawn to our Lord as they see us loving each other (see John 13:34–35). Love is best demonstrated as we sacrificially serve each other.

♦ We are an empowered people. God has empowered all believers with the indwelling Holy Spirit in order to serve Him (see Acts 1:8). Empowering people in our churches means trusting our people to become engaged in ministry without a lot of controls.

♦ The prime role of leaders is to give ministry away to others. A contemporary rendering of Ephesians 4:11–12 might say, "for the empowering of the saints for the work of ministry."

♦ The Exodus Principle is a manual to consult time and time again for ideas on how to empower people for service in our churches.

————

Something to Think About

The heart of a healthy church is found in sacrificial service to those inside and outside the church.

————

Evaluating Your Spirit of Service

1. Do people in your church go out of their way to serve each other? ( ) YES   ( ) NO

2. Do people in your church give of themselves beyond normal expectations? ( ) YES   ( ) NO

3. Do people in your church exhibit a spirit of generosity toward each other? ( ) YES   ( ) NO

4. Do people often express appreciation for care they have received from others in your church? ( ) YES   ( ) NO

5. Do visitors sense a spirit of love and care?
   ( ) YES ( ) NO
   _____

How Well Are You Empowering People?

Think back over the last three to five years and make a quick list of all the new ministries that have been started in or through your church during that time.

Having made your list, divide them under the following two categories. Category A: Ministries primarily initiated and directed by a staff or board member. Category B: Ministries primarily initiated and directed by a layperson.

Category A

_____

_____

_____

_____

_____

_____

_____

_____

Category B

_____
_____
_____
_____
_____

1. Under which category do most of your new ministries fall?_____

_____
_____

2. How easy is it for a layperson to initiate and direct a new ministry in your church?_____

_____
_____

3. How difficult is it for a person to begin a new ministry in your church?_____

_____
_____

4. What are the main obstacles to overcome in freeing people up to become involved in personal ministry?____

_____
_____

5. What creative changes need to be made to empower lay members to start some new ministries in the next few years?_____

_____
_____

PART ONE

Designing a Culture of Service

CHAPTER ONE

Create a Culture

Most churches are steeped in culture. It can be positive, negative, or nondescript, but even a seeming lack of culture is in and of itself a culture. Although I didn't totally comprehend the concept of culture at the time, when I was in college I served as a youth pastor, music director, and pastoral assistant in three different churches, each with a very distinct culture.

The first was a small neighborhood church hidden in a middle-class suburb of Denver, Colorado. The people who attended appreciated the family atmosphere where everyone was accepted and loved. Members generally walked to church or drove from within a few miles of the building. Although the Bible was taught, doctrine was not a major emphasis of the teaching. People had agreed to accept the basics of the Christian faith and not fight over what they called non-essentials. Maintaining the "small-church feel" was valued more than reaching new people in the community. The door of the church was always open, and new people were accepted when they came; but few showed up.

The second church I served was in a farming community of 25,000. Our church was on a corner, and some visited the worship services because of the high visibility of our building to drive-by traffic. Deep doctrinal studies of the Bible were common in the worship service, Sunday School, and home Bible studies. Every new person soon discovered that he or she must know or get to know the Bible. New believers, or those with limited Bible knowledge, often felt uncomfortable attempting to participate in discussions with more knowledgeable members. Reaching the community for Christ was left to college interns who canvassed homes door-to-door in the immediate neighborhood inviting people to church.

The third church I served demonstrated a strong interest in evangelism. The pastor led the way by visiting many non-churched people to share the gospel with them. All committed leaders were expected to participate in the weeknight visitation ministry. Members were regularly admonished and exhorted from the pulpit to witness to their non-Christian friends and family members. After attending for a few weeks, new worshipers discovered the church had a very strict code of conduct that restrained them from doing certain activities the leaders had determined were unacceptable for Christians. Messages focused on living the Christian life as a witness to neighbors, coworkers, and family members.

These short descriptions point out that churches are more than buildings, programs, and budgets. Each church is a living body of Christ, and each community of faith has a distinct culture or personality similar to that of individual people. Each church has a different set of behaviors, values, and beliefs, and an atmosphere that sets it apart from other churches, even those of like faith and practice. I'm sure you noted the different cultures in the three churches I described. Undoubtedly you can also name churches you've attended and describe their varying cultures.

Four Elements of a Church's Culture

Culture is at once a simple and complex concept. However, it is not my purpose in this book to delve into the intricacies of culture. Culture is nothing more than the behaviors, values, rules, and atmosphere a group of people share. From the perspective of a local church, culture is simply "the way we do church around here."[1] The system or "way we do church" is often described by understanding four elements of culture.

Element 1: Behaviors

Each church has its own systematic routines of everyday life. These behaviors are referred to as rites, rituals, and ceremonies. All the activities of a church—worshiping, practicing communion, electing church officers, handling conflict, and other behaviors—communicate a lot about what a church is really like.

Element 2: Values

The values are the basic concepts or beliefs of a church. These values may be written or unwritten and are extremely powerful in forming the heart of church culture. Very few churches take the time to identify and write down their values but, as an example, a church might value creativity or conformity, flexibility or rigidness, tolerance or intolerance, keeping up with the times or holding to the past. Unrecognized values are stumbling blocks to anyone attempting to engineer a new church culture.

Element 3: Rules

Each organization has its own standardized ways of operating. These rules are normally written down and include the church doctrinal statement, constitution and bylaws, articles of incorporation, and any written policy statements—weddings, facilities usage, and others.

Element 4: Atmosphere

All cultures have a basic feel about them, and each church culture has its own feel or atmosphere. People, especially newcomers, catch a sense of the overall feel of a church within thirty to sixty seconds of entering a church building on Sunday morning. There are innumerable possibilities of how a church culture may feel. One church may have the atmosphere of excitement, joy, victory, or love, while another church may have the bitter feel of discouragement, defeat, or criticism. A culture of service is, at the most basic aspect, more experience than anything else.

_____

A church's culture may be very strong and easy to describe, or fairly weak and difficult to pinpoint. Yet no matter how strong or weak, a church's culture exists and affects practically everything the church does. It has a major effect on a church's growth and decline, on which new programs succeed and which programs fail, on who gets elected to church offices and who does not. The church is people, and people make churches work. Each church's culture ties the people together and gives them meaning in their ministry.

Ten Steps to Building a New Culture

A major part of a church leader's role is to build a church culture that empowers people to live out Christian lives of service. There are no magical formulas. In many cases it will take some trial and error to arrive at a strong church culture that empowers people to be all that God wants them to be. Some leaders think they can simply give a "state of the church" address in January which says, "We will have a new culture around here now," and it will happen. Others feel that a new set of plans should do the trick. Some try to dictate a new culture of service and then blame others when it doesn't take root.

A new culture of service will come into existence only when there is a reason for it to exist. It will exist when the total atmosphere expresses values of service and concern for the individual. It will exist when there is a plan for it. All we need is a clear and meaningful vision of what the organization must accomplish, a strategy for the journey, a clear set of values to guide the way, and a form of leadership that trusts people enough to give them the power to work passionately. It is important to develop a strategy. Overlooking strategy and rushing headlong to develop a culture of service is always a mistake because strategy defines the steps along the way.

Here are some steps that others have used to build strong church cultures. I offer them to help you start building a culture of service. Every chapter of this book will focus on defining and enlarging on our understanding of serving others. It will be good for us, however, to begin thinking strategically at this point.

Step 1: Commit to the Long Haul

Church cultures are notoriously slow to build and hard to change. Culture is an attitude that takes at least five to seven years to build up. It takes a lot of coaching, leadership, and example-setting to see it become reality. Part of the difficulty lies in the fact that culture is a "soft" subject. Budgets, plans, and buildings are all "hard" subjects which can be touched, read and reviewed. Certain aspects of church culture—attitudes, feelings, and perceptions—are all "soft" subjects and are much more difficult to get a handle on. If you want to change your church's culture, you must commit to the long haul.

When I was a child, my dad would drive into a service station. That is what he got—service. Smiling, uniformed men would pump gas, check oil, air up tires, and wash *windows. They could perform repairs and tune-ups. I could get air for my bicycle, use the rest room, and buy a Coke.*

Nowadays, an attendant sits behind bulletproof glass. There is seldom a smile or greeting or "thank you." No free air, and if you want gas or a clean windshield, you'll have to do it yourself. Signs no longer say Service; they say Fuel.

Churches have the name, but do they offer "service" in Jesus' name as He told us to do? Do we serve the sick and dying? Do we serve the hungry and poorly clothed? If we do not serve in His name, perhaps, we should have at least as much integrity as the gas stations and change our name to more correctly describe our work.

—Stephen Earle, First Baptist Church, Ponca City, Oklahoma, as quoted in *Illustration Digest* (June-August 1993), 14.

Step 2: Help Members Understand Culture

Church leaders must have an understanding of church culture and a specific understanding of what their church's culture currently is like. Church leaders are often "hard" subject types of people. They may ignore the "soft" aspects of culture and be much more adept at dealing with "hard" items such as budgets, plans, and buildings. Part of the reason it takes five to seven years to engineer a new church culture is that leaders must be educated to understand it and see it.

Step 3: Draw a Picture of Your Current Church Culture

You must tap into the knowledge of the people who "live" your present church culture. Spend time formally and informally asking questions, identifying values, and discovering your way of doing things. Search below the surface to identify the unwritten values and rules that presently drive your church. What do your behaviors, values, rules, and atmosphere say about your church? How do members and non-members see your church? Be ruthlessly honest in your description. This is no time to fool yourself. Draw a picture of your present church culture and identify what needs to be held on to and what new cultural values people would like to see come into existence.

Step 4: Mold a New Church Culture

Spend a lot of time with your people, dreaming as a group. Read passages in the Bible that describe what a church should be and then verbalize a new cultural vision for your church based on what you learned. What type of atmosphere do you want newcomers to feel when they visit you? What do you want people to say about your church when they talk to others? What values do your people naturally buy into? Your people are on the front lines and, if given the opportunity, will help mold a new culture of service for the future. What do you want your new culture to be like in the future?

You should also take the time to visit churches that are doing a superb job of serving their people. Nothing will help you more than experiencing what others are doing. Call a hundred people in your community and ask them which churches are the best ones. Then visit each church that is mentioned, taking notes, talking to people, and sensing the atmosphere. You may borrow some ideas, adapt some, and even reject others. It can be one of the best things you can do to enlarge your people's vision of what can be done at your own church. Before you can think about designing a new culture of service, you must decide how good you want to be. Do you want to provide the best service?

Step 5: Formalize Your New Culture

You begin to formalize your new culture by creating an official mission statement and a set of philosophies and values. Calling people to a new culture of service will only take place when people understand and feel a sense of passion for the mission or purpose of their church.

The Apollo space project called Americans to a "great and worthwhile challenge, something so new and spectacular as to dazzle the imagination, and it was something to be proud of."[2] It began on May 25, 1961, when President John F. Kennedy set a goal to land a man on the moon and return him safely to earth by the end of that decade. The Apollo missions caught the attention of the American public and reached its peak on July 20, 1969, when astronaut Neil Armstrong stepped out of the Apollo 11 lunar module *Eagle* and set foot on the moon. The vision and culture of achievement set in motion by President Kennedy only eight years earlier was completed.

To establish a new culture of service may take a type of Apollo project to awaken people to the possibilities of a new direction. Karl Albrecht believes that people commit themselves to a new direction, and he calls this the "Apollo effect."

A specific challenge or project in your church that reflects your new cultural values will cause people to feel committed again, to feel good about being involved in something worthwhile. People only give their energies to something when they know, understand, and believe in their mission. You may even want to give your new culture a new name. Strong cultures have slogans that mean something. Yet don't be fooled into thinking that a new slogan will change things. *Slogans mean nothing without actions that support them.* Empty words that find no correlation between the slogans and statements of mission, values, and philosophy with the true culture will breed cynicism. Too many slogans and too little action is not good.

Step 6: Model the New Culture

Leaders are crucial to culture. Their words and deeds are the touchstones of a church's culture. Creating a positive culture of service means demonstrating concern for people already in the church, enhancing their dignity, and solving their problems quickly and fairly.

Little things will make a big difference in a leader's ability to convince others of the seriousness of the new culture. For example, if a church leader asks members to park farther away from the church in order to leave space for newcomers but then keeps his own "official" parking space near the church, he should not be surprised that members will not accept the new culture of service.

Step 7: Communicate Your New Culture

Never try to force your new culture on people. Rather, concentrate on making steady inroads by communicating your new culture of service in a regular manner. You can do this in several ways:

- Introduce your new culture in a formal manner by kicking it off with a churchwide meeting. Anything this important calls for a face-to-face meeting of everyone.

- Rename key people or aspects of your church to communicate a new status and value to them. Some church leaders have even started calling church members "pastors" in an effort to communicate a new status to them that fits a new culture.

- Require that all new members take an orientation class on your church. Spend the bulk of the time in the class communicating the values and behaviors of your new culture of service.

- Train a team of five people who truly understand and believe in your new culture of service and have them visit as many groups and classes as possible to train others.

- Make display cards for persons in your church to keep on their desk at work or table at home with statements that communicate the values of your new culture of service.

+ Laminate wallet cards with your mission statement, philosophies, and values on them and give one to every person
in your church to carry.

Step 8: Reinforce Your New Culture

Use your church's newsletter to reinforce your culture by
sharing stories of how members illustrate the new culture.
Interview people from the pulpit who are excellent examples
or can give testimonials supporting the values of the new
culture. Write personal letters to key people enlarging upon
the importance of cultural values.

Step 9: Recognize People Who Embody New Cultural Values

Give an award or flowers or a specially designed pin to
those who demonstrate great commitment to your cultural
values. To be highly successful, recognition must take place
more than once a year. It needs to take place whenever
someone goes above and beyond to serve another person. Call
the office staff together to recognize office personnel. Go into
a Sunday School class to award a class member. Recognize
people as quickly as possible in a public manner so that others
see that you believe in your cultural values. Be sure to use the
most powerful recognition available—a personal note of
thanks. Whenever you hear of persons in your church who
made a major contribution to the overall culture you are
trying to develop, send them a handwritten note of thanks.
It's better than an award.

Step 10: Celebrate Your Church Culture

Host an annual churchwide event to highlight your culture of service. This is a once-a-year meeting, and it must be
fun and exciting. Bringing everyone together creates an atmosphere that is hard to duplicate. It builds morale and
reinforces your culture of service. Take the opportunity to

highlight your mission and values to everyone present. Give out several service awards and celebrate the blessing of God on your church during the past year.

Turning on the Power

To empower people in a new culture of service is a great idea. It is difficult, however, to get people to work with commitment and passion when their leaders don't trust them and tend to overcontrol them. Many church leaders think that empowerment means giving people a tiny bit more freedom of action in certain specific situations. However, people in our church can handle much more than we as leaders allow them.

Many people already have the information, authority, and training to deal with major issues in their jobs and lives, but when it comes to church we often try to dominate them. What turns the power of culture on in a church? The answer begins with leadership.

People who lead with a spirit of service in their own hearts and minds will attract followers with the same spirit. Leaders who lord it over others will attract followers who are self-centered rather than service-centered. People who are self-centered are too busy looking after their own needs or fighting for status to commit themselves to serving others. Visitors to a church usually pick up a feeling from the people already attending a church.

If there is a spirit of anger or resentment in the congregation, it will translate into apathy or even hostility toward newcomers no matter how much one tries to disguise it. On the other hand, if there is a spirit of teamwork and care for each other, it will translate into genuine interest in and concern for the needs of new people. Feelings and attitudes are contagious. The way your members and regular attenders feel will ultimately be the way newcomers feel about your church.

True Colors Will Shine Through

My stepfather was a house painter, and I learned enough of the trade from him to feel comfortable painting my own house. In my experience, I've found it difficult to paint over dark colors. Once when I painted my son's room, I attempted to cover dark blue with an off-white. Even after two coats of paint the color underneath kept bleeding through.

Engineering a new church culture is like painting over a darker color. The original culture will keep bleeding through unless people truly accept the new culture. You can write a new mission statement and develop a new slogan, but it's not the language; it's attitude. It's easy to write a new constitution and bylaws, but what makes them meaningful is that the people are willing to back them up with action. It's the depth behind the statements that counts. People's true colors will bleed through, and so will your church's. Capturing a new culture of service is only totally successful when the hearts of your regular worshipers are committed to a new spirit of sacrificial service.

Capturing a Culture—A Summary

- Culture is a simple and complex concept. A culture is a system of behaviors, values, rules, and atmosphere that a group of people share.

- A church's culture may be broken down into four elements.

  1. behaviors: general actions, rites, rituals, and ceremonies

  2. values: written or unwritten beliefs

  3. rules: constitutions, by-laws, and doctrinal statements

  4. atmosphere: the general feel of the church

- A major role of church leaders is to understand their church's current culture and design a culture of service that empowers people to serve both inside and outside the church.

♦ There are no magical formulas, but there are steps that will help bring a new culture of service into existence.

1. Commit to the long haul.

2. Help members understand culture.

3. Draw a picture of your current church culture.

4. Mold a new church culture.

5. Formalize your new culture.

6. Model the new culture.

7. Communicate your new culture.

8. Reinforce your new culture.

9. Recognize people who embody new cultural values.

10. Celebrate your church culture.

♦ Attitudes are contagious. The way your church members and regular worshipers feel about their church will ultimately be the way newcomers feel about your church.

♦ A church's true colors will shine through. Writing a new mission statement, establishing new philosophies, and designing plans are important. Yet it's not the language; it's the attitude behind the language. It's the depth behind the statements that count. It's the people willing to back up the words with action that give power to a new culture of service.

———

Something to Think About

A church's culture affects practically everything a church does.

———

Your Paramount Belief

Churches that exhibit a strong culture often summarize their culture with a slogan-like statement. What slogan or statement best characterizes your church's cultural values? _____

_____

How successfully does your church fulfill its slogan?____

_____

_____

Conduct a Cultural Audit

1. What key values form the major foundation of your church's culture? _____

_____

2. Do people in your church know these values?_____

_____

_____

If so, who knows them? How many? Who does not know them? _____

_____

3. How do these values affect day-to-day decisions?____

_____

_____

_____

4. How are these values communicated to your people?

_____

_____

_____

5. How many of these values would your people name if you asked them?_____

_____

_____

CHAPTER TWO

Put People First

*P*utting people first doesn't always come naturally. In the early growth years of the automobile industry, Henry Ford set the standards by using mass production techniques and standardized parts. He found that by building one type of car he could produce them quickly and cheaply. His Model T was affordable, met most people's needs, and it made Ford Motor Company the major automobile manufacturer of the time.

It didn't stay that way for long. Gradually people started asking for different models and colors of cars. Unfortunately, Henry Ford was not interested in putting people first. His response to people's requests for different colors was, "People can buy any color car they want, as long as it's black." His lack of putting people first caused Ford Motor Company to fall from its number one position in car manufacturing as it lost market shares to General Motors.

If your church wants to engineer a new culture of service, you must put people first. This is only common sense. Service is a social process, a web of interactions among people.

Putting people first tends to reinforce the desire and commitment of people to serve each other. This phenomenon is called the "virtuous circle," meaning that when people are put first they tend to feel more satisfied with their church. They communicate with others and tend to put other people first in their own contacts, thus keeping the circle of service flowing from one person to another.

Who Is Our Customer?

The Peter F. Drucker Foundation suggests that all nonprofit organizations (including churches) need to ask an important question: "Who is our customer?" Granted, most of us are not accustomed to thinking of people who attend or visit our church as customers. A customer is someone who buys something from us on a regular basis. This usage doesn't fit the church well since we are not selling anything. Our church is in the service business. We serve others by giving them the free gospel of Jesus Christ.

The term customer, however, can also refer to those with whom we have regular contact. This is an appropriate usage for the church since we do have dealings with people. Perhaps the term *constituency*, referring to those who together make up the broad group of people we serve through our church, fits the church better. Actually every company or organization has its own unique term for customer. Doctors call them patients, attorneys call them clients, and churches call them members and guests. Yet no matter which term we choose to use, serving people is what churches are called to do.

To do the best job of putting people first, we must identify and understand the people we serve. A startling example of this is found in Acts 6. The church in Jerusalem was growing quickly and the people had organized a fairly good means of serving one another. Most were extremely happy, but one group was being overlooked. The Hellenistic Jews felt that their widows were not being served well by the church. The disciples and other church leaders made the mistake of thinking that they had only one group of customers when, in fact, they had two very different groups of people expecting to be served. By identifying a different segment of people, the disciples were able to develop a plan to serve all their constituents well. They were able to put people first in their church because they had identified their different needs and expectations and adjusted their ministry to serve them.

Internal Customers

Every church has at least two main customers to be served: people in the church and people outside the church. Our internal customers are those who already call our church "home," whether they are members or regular worshipers. They are easily identified and served. We probably already have their names and addresses in our church records. What's more, the weekly contact we have with each other gives us inside clues on how to serve each other.

External Customers

Our external customers are people who could attend our church if the appropriate circumstance existed. These external customers represent a group that is at the very least six times larger than our internal customer group. They are the friends, family members, and acquaintances of our worshipers. They are the people who drive by our church daily on their way to work. They are the people we are trying to reach with the good news of Jesus Christ.

On Whom Should We Focus?

Since we have two groups of customers—internal and external—where do we place the priority in our efforts at putting people first? It's not always an easy question to answer. Christ called to us to care for each other inside the church as well as reach the lost. It's not an either/or situation but a both/and situation. Yet in practice we have to begin by placing the emphasis on one group or the other in the initial stages of engineering a culture of service.

In most cases, it's best to begin by focusing on people inside our church. I discovered this while pastoring a church in Portland, Oregon. I had arrived at the church with the intention of focusing on outreach and evangelism. After getting acquainted with the people, I soon learned that little fellowship or support had taken place among the members for several years.

One evening as the deacons and I were preparing to visit some church members, I specifically asked the chairman of our deacons to ride with me to the homes of some members. My desire was twofold. I wanted to get to know this deacon better. I also thought he would know most of the people, could direct me to their homes, and introduce me to those I had not already met. I handed him three cards with the names and addresses of members I wanted to visit.

He glanced through the cards, looked at me, and commented, "Pastor, I don't know where any of these people live." Surprised, I replied that I thought after so many years at the church he would know everyone (the church wasn't very big). Embarrassed, he mumbled back, "Pastor, I've been in this church fifteen years, but I've never been in the home of any other church members but those of my own family."

Before I could lead this church in reaching out to its external customers, I needed to help the members begin putting each other first in their own church. How could they effectively put outsiders first when they couldn't even talk to each other in their own homes? If our internal customers feel good about our church and know how to care for each other,

then they will do a better job of serving our external customers. Many churches just starting to build a culture of service
will find putting people first means focusing on building care
among those already in the church.

Some churches may find that they have a congregation
that knows how to love and care for each other. Their
people are putting each other first in very practical ways.
In such a case, it will be better to place the emphasis on
those outside the church. But unless this is the case, it will
do no good to reach out to people and attempt to bring
them into a church that doesn't demonstrate the values you
hope to convey. Newcomers will see through such hypoc-
risy quickly.

How to Put People First

Putting people first means treating people the way they
expect to be treated. Your mother was right. It is best to treat
people with courtesy and respect. If we hope to build a
church culture that offers excellent service, we need to be
polite.

Putting people first is not just a program, it's an attitude,
a way of life. As such, putting people first means we listen to
them. This means taking the time to talk informally with
people as well as being reasonably available to them for
appointments. It means taking their concerns seriously and
responding appropriately.

We put people first when we provide ministry on their
time schedules. If people are working Sunday, we may provide
a service for them on a weeknight. Do we do everything a
person wants? Of course not. It must fit our mission and
philosophy of ministry. We must have the resources to do it.
We may have to admit honestly that we'd like to accommodate
them, but at this time we simply can't do it. Our intent

throughout, however, is to serve by putting people first as much as we possibly can.

Too often we forget that issues are people. We throw up our hands at our inability to affect the debate. Yet by remembering that behind every issue, no matter how important or controversial, are real people—people whom Christ loves and longs to have a relationship with—we can have an impact.

In the 1960s, no issue was more controversial than school desegregation. Following a Sunday morning service, a woman stopped me and mentioned that she and her husband had attended the church for a few weeks and enjoyed the services. She said that her husband was not a Christian but respected me. I asked what her husband did, and she told me that he worked for the school district. She also mentioned that as a result of his responsibilities he was at the very center of the community's school integration issue. I told her that I would like to meet her husband. We arranged for the three of us to have lunch.

The lunch lasted almost two hours. I listened to the burdens of a man whose name was in the public debate daily. I asked about his relationship with Christ. He stated that he was a self-made man, who at thirty-five had never considered Jesus. I asked him if he was afraid that if he accepted Jesus Christ, he would become bored. He nodded yes. I then asked him to share with me the last two weeks of his life. I then shared with him the last two weeks of my life and told him that I found the Christian life anything but boring. He soon had to return to work, so he excused himself. I stayed and spent a little more time with his wife. She asked if I was aware of what had just happened. She said that her husband was never at a loss for words; but after he and I had finished comparing schedules, he was quiet. Too quiet.

A couple of weeks later, the man at the center of the most controversial issue of his day came to Christ. He and I spent time together. Although in the midst of heavy responsibilities and a heightened workload due to an impending federal court hearing, he made time to read the Bible. In fact, in his first four months as a Christian he read from Genesis to Jeremiah. I was with him in the courtroom as the hearing began. At a break just prior to when he would be called to the witness stand to explain and defend his work, we walked down the hall and slipped into a corner to pray. Upon our return, he took the stand to begin his testimony.

What is community? It is people—people whom God invites us to come alongside. What do godly men and women do in community? They come alongside one another, and they pray. Who is someone in your community you might call today or reach out to and extend the friendship of Christ? What issues are you praying about? Who has God put into your life to pray for?

How has God made your life exciting in the past two weeks?

"God created" (Gen. 1:1); "You are the light of the world" (Matt. 5:14).

–Chuck Miller, pastor, Celebration Community Church; in
What Makes a Man? Bill McCartney et al. (NavPress), 174–75,
used by permission.

We put people first when we provide them a phone number to call in case of emergencies. In a smaller church, all members should have the home phone numbers of the pastoral staff and church leaders. When a church gets larger, a senior pastor should give his home phone number to executive staff and main board members. Associate staff should give their phone numbers to people directly under their oversight or on committees that serve their ministry function. Small group leaders must give their phone numbers to the people in their small groups. Putting people first means we give people a way to get in touch with someone when they have a need. You should want people to call you, no matter what time it is. They're your customers, and you need to serve them. Their call gives you a chance to maintain your relationship with them, and people really like you to serve them this way. Don't worry about people taking advantage of you. As a rule, they'll only call if they honestly need help.

We put people first when we appreciate them. Most churches send a letter to visitors thanking them for attending, but how often do we thank our regular attenders for being faithful? Both are important ways to put people first. Whenever you learn that someone has gone out of their way to serve another person in your church, make certain it gets written up and made known. If you have a church newsletter, you can put a story in it. If not, try this. Write up the act of service, have it framed and give it to the other person. Read the story to everyone present. Giving an award in this manner highlights the act of service that was accomplished and holds up your values for everyone to see.

You put people first when you serve their needs. Recognize that you cannot meet every need nor every expectation; therefore, you must prioritize the needs and expectations you will attempt to meet. First, identify the three things that are most important to each group. Once you know what is important, you can then provide it. In practice, evangelism is targeted to external customers and focuses on their needs. In contrast, developing a culture of service to members already in the church should focus on meeting their expectations.

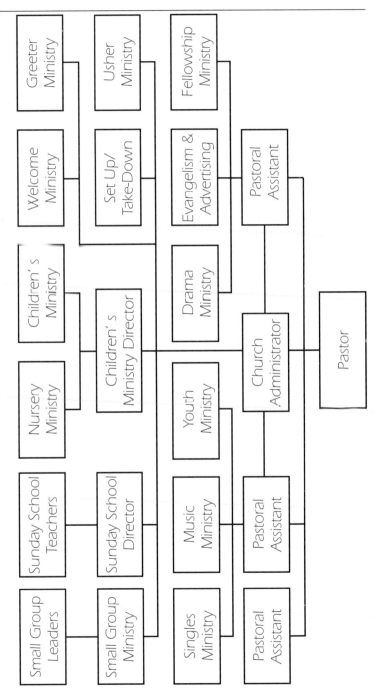

We put people first when we build our church in a way that stresses the frontline importance of people and their ministry. One way to illustrate that people are first is to use the inverted pyramid with frontline people at the top and leaders at the bottom (see the illustration on p. 38). Most organizational charts in churches place the pastor at the top, followed by staff or board members, followed by those who are serving in each area. A top-down chart gives the impression that the people at the top are the most important people in their church's ministry. In this chart people who are on the front lines of ministry are put first.

Churches that perceive unbelievers as their primary customers may find a concentric chart (below) communicates their idea of serving people outside the church best. New people are placed in the bull's-eye—the most valuable position—those closest to them in the next ring, on out to the last ring which is the paid staff. This is not a true organizational chart showing reporting relationships or functional divisions and organizational structure. Instead, the concentric chart

tells everyone that the purpose of the church is to reach the unchurched. All decisions are to be made based on reaching the unchurched, which is why they are put first.

No church can put people first unless the pastoral staff and main leaders visibly and constantly commit themselves to the idea. Putting people first gets done only if the people at the top lead the charge. When they don't set the example, everyone succumbs to the pressure of just "doing" church instead of serving one another.

When a church lacks unremitting evidence from the top that a culture of service is important, the daily, unglamorous job of serving each other loses out to the desire to be served. One lady who was a leader in her church set an excellent example of service. She considered it a ministry to sit in a different place each week for the worship service, becoming acquainted with those who sat in that area. She often discovered lonely people—and the means by which they could be drawn into greater service in the church. Having suffered through a life-threatening illness herself, she understood others' needs and often would go out of her way to sacrificially serve those she met. This woman put people first.

It's no surprise that having a champion at the top is crucial to implementing a culture of service in a church. The same could be said of any strategy: All of them need to be defended against competing pressures, all will be ignored unless leaders make them important. Leaders should place a sign on their desks that reads, "Who have I put first today?"

Serving Our Customers—A Summary

♦   Putting people first creates a virtuous circle. As people are served in the church, they in turn communicate their satisfaction about their church to others and put others first.

♦ Every church has two main customers to serve: people inside the church, and people outside the church. We must strive for a balance in serving both of these groups.

♦ If a church does not have a solid history of sacrificial service, it is best to focus on building a spirit of service among internal customers—church members. If those already in your church learn how to serve each other, they will do a better job of serving those outside the church.

♦ In the broadest sense, putting people first means to treat them in the manner which they expect to be treated. There are many practical ways this can be fulfilled.

♦ Using an inverted pyramid is a good tool to illustrate a new way of looking at a church's organizational structure from a service point of view.

Something to Think About

A secret of building a culture of service in a local church is to put people first.

Thinking It Through

Putting people first is both an attitude and a process. What is your church's attitude about putting people first? Can you identify specific actions or incidents that illustrate this attitude? _____

_____

_____

Are there ministries, programs, or other organizational processes in place in your church that communicate or help ensure that people are put first in your ministry?___

_____

_____

_____

What are they? What new structures could you begin to develop to help reinforce this value?_____

_____

_____

_____

Telling Your Story

Find one story that illustrates the value of putting people first in your church's ministry. Write it into a short illustration that you can share with the entire congregation.

If there are people still present in your church who were the ones sacrificially serving others in your story, give them a framed copy in front of the congregation after you read it.

Use the story over and over again so that it becomes well known and a symbol of your church's legendary commitment to putting people first.

_____

CHAPTER THREE

Trust People to Serve

It was Carthage, North Africa, in A.D. 252 that the bubonic plague terrorized the city. Death raced from door to door. The odor was horrifying. People resisted helping each other for fear of attracting the disease themselves. However, a local church committed to a culture of service made a strategic investment in the lives of the citizens of Carthage. These people chose to put their lives on the line for the cause of Christ. They called themselves "parabolani"—the risk-takers. They followed the courageous model of Epaphroditus in Philippians 2:25–27, and their loving acts of service impacted an entire city. History records the decisive fact that Carthage was saved from destruction because of the risk-takers of the church.

Our Lord did not call us to Carthage, instead He has placed us in our present location for the purpose of giving sacrificial service to those both inside and outside our churches today. To be sure, risks we face are different than they were for the church in Carthage, but any church seriously involved in serving others must take risks.

Spiritual risk is the healthy child of biblical faith. It is the day-to-day, responsible, obedient action of the Christian and the church motivated by God's love and grace. That's our business—honoring God by having enough faith to take some risks in the process of developing a culture of service in our church.

Serving others does involve risks. I remember receiving a phone call late at night from a risk-taker in my church. Bev had been visiting friends. While walking to her car to leave, she caught sight of a woman sitting on suitcases in front of the house next door. Seeing an opportunity to serve, Bev approached the woman to offer her a ride.

The woman's drinking had led to her being kicked out of the house by her family. She had a car but could not drive and had no place to stay. At this point, Bev called me for help. We decided the best way to serve the woman was to provide her with a place to stay for the evening. I met them and then drove the woman to a local motel, with Bev following behind in her own car.

Arriving at the motel I entered the lobby with the woman at my side and received a very cold reception from the attendant. Apparently, he thought I was with that woman for a purpose other than a room. Fortunately Bev arrived and, with a sense of embarrassment, we explained the situation and were able to rent a room for the woman. Looking back at the incident, I was very naive and put my reputation in danger. Yet Bev was a risk-taker and, for that evening, had made me one too.

Invest in People

Investors don't make fortunes by worrying about the daily direction of the stock market. They believe in a growing economy, and they buy stocks that will accurately represent that future. Risk is a part of their investment decision. Those who invest well reap huge rewards. Those who make wrong predictions of the future lose. Yet the biggest losers are often those who fail to take any risk, for while they limit their potential for loss, they also have no chance to gain anything.

A friend of mine says there are three kinds of leaders in the church: risk-takers, caretakers, and undertakers. The undertakers belong to churches that show great fear of serving others. The caretakers risk enough to serve each other but won't go beyond the people of their own church. The risk-takers courageously lead their people to serve each other and those in the community.

The most challenging risk that leaders often have to take is investing the ministry in their people. Even though we know that the clergy-laity gap is unbiblical, putting into practice the truth that we are all servants of Christ has proven difficult. Too many pastors and other church leaders hold their people down, fearing the mistakes they might make if given freedom to serve. I'm reminded of this difficulty when I try to help church leaders begin a small-group ministry. They unfailingly want to select leaders for their small groups from people who are already too involved in church activities to do a good job. When I suggest they select leaders from people who are not yet involved, their reaction is predictable. They fear the outcomes of placing new people in places of ministry. Letting their fears run wild, they become emotionally blocked from empowering new people with a chance at ministry and end up keeping ministry in the hands of a few trusted and overworked leaders.

Not so in a culture of service. In a culture of service, ministry is everyone's business—we all become risk-takers. Unless everyone in the church assumes responsibility for serving each other, a culture of service dies. Leaders are risk-takers encouraging every member to bring their actions and behaviors into agreement with what God has made them—a minister of Christ.

Support Their Ideas

One of the surest ways to empower people to serve is to uphold their ideas. If any church member approaches you with an idea for a ministry, the answer must always be yes! Does this mean your church sanctions every ministry idea a person wishes to attempt? No, it doesn't. Then how should you support their idea?

Praise risk-takers for coming up with such an idea. You may think the idea is dumb, but at least they have taken the risk of approaching you with a creative idea. That's outstanding. How many more ideas do you think they will come to you with if you criticize this one? If you can't praise their idea, at least praise them for being creative and courageous enough to think of it.

Ask risk-takers to find five other people willing to team with them to help build such a ministry. Have them schedule a meeting with you when their team has been assembled. Doing this has many advantages. It empowers them to begin working on their idea. It requires them to define and communicate their vision for ministry well enough to attract others to it. It allows others in the church to confirm, refine, or reject the ministry idea.

When you meet with the team, let them know how enthusiastic you are to learn of their commitment and willingness to serve. Encourage them to think through how the new ministry fits with your mission and direction as a church. They should especially think through how their new idea fits with your culture of service.

Support risk-takers with all the training they need but encourage them to find their own funding. Leaders are responsible to provide training (see Eph. 4:12) but not necessarily to provide financial assistance. Placing responsibility for funding the ministry on the team developing it ensures that only ministries with a large enough vision to attract funding will likely be started. This is another way of verifying the appropriateness of the new ministry.

Assure risk-takers that the church will support them in every possible way. This especially means promoting their ministry through your church if they abide by four guidelines:

1. The new ministry must maintain legal, moral, and ethical integrity.

2. The new ministry must be biblically based and doctrinally in agreement with your church.

3. The leaders of the new ministry must attend your church's ongoing leadership training events.

4. The leaders of the group must present to the church leadership a record of how many people attend their ministry, what is going well, and what difficulties they are experiencing.

Taking the risk to empower people for ministry in this way will take a few years to develop. If your response to ideas for new ministries has always been no, it will take a few years to convince them that you are serious. Once you prove to them that you are willing to be a risk-taker and allow them to begin their own ministries, people will approach you for encouragement, direction, and training.

In the beginning stages of building your culture of service, it is not likely that you will find a large number of people standing in line to discuss a new ministry they want to start. Thus, you will need to establish a systematic way to recruit, train, and motivate people to serve.

Recruiting People for Service

Getting people involved in an area of service seems simple enough: recruit the right people, train them, and keep them motivated. But doing so in practice is extraordinarily difficult—too difficult for many leaders to master, apparently. Part of the challenge is because of the way we have traditionally recruited people for ministry. Institutional-based recruiting worked well when the United States was a church-going culture. Years ago people attended church from a sense of duty. When the church issued a call for service, people responded because it was the correct thing to do. If the church needed a third-grade Sunday School teacher, the pastor would announce the need from the pulpit and someone would volunteer to fill the position. An institution-based recruitment strategy emphasizes the institution's need more than the need of the individual. The church (institution) needs a third-grade teacher. Yet does the individual need to serve?

An institution-based recruitment strategy doesn't work well today. Most people no longer attend church out of a sense of duty, nor do they serve from a sense of duty. Churches in today's world must use a relation-based recruitment strategy—a strategy that emphasizes needs of the individual more than the needs of the institution.

One-by-One Method

In a culture of service, the best way to recruit people is to start by serving them and their interests. You will need to recruit people one-by-one using an interview approach. Use what is termed a "behavioral interview," seeking to discover what experience (or behavior) individuals have had involving frequent contact with others. In what ways have they served people before? How did they enjoy it?

In addition, get to know the persons. What are their gifts, interests, and talents? The object of the interview is not to fill a need at your church but to get to know the individual. Once this has been accomplished, then potential ministry opportunities for service may be offered to the person based on what you discovered during the interview. Attempt to match the person with the service opportunity so that there is a good fit.

Encourage people to make their own decisions for ministry. Ask them to select a ministry that sounds interesting to them or one for which they have some passion.

Churches with a strong culture of service work to find the right people for the right place of service. Select people whose personalities are predisposed to provide the kind of service you want to express in your church. A few months ago I was walking though a shopping center when I noticed a sign in a store window about a job opening. Underneath in large letters was highlighted, "We hire friendly people." The manager of this store had some inside information: It's easier to hire friendly people than to train people to be friendly. It's also easier to recruit people who agree with your church's values than to hire those who don't and try to change their values later on. You can't teach people to be nice. You can't just say, "Monday morning, begin caring for others." Caring and serving others must be inherent in their hearts.

Recruit to a team; never place people in a ministry alone. People serving together in teams respond to ministry opportunities better than those working alone. In times of discouragement they support one another. At other times they hold each other accountable to fulfill their calling. People prefer reporting to each other than to a boss.

Recruit to a project that has a limited time span. The basic principle: Recruit for the short-term and renew for the long-term. A culture of service also declares war on bureaucracy. So keep policies, procedures, and formal control mechanisms to a minimum, relying instead on cultural control and people's commitment to their team to control the ministry.

Train, Train, Train

In 1968 I began working for Radio Shack. At the time I knew very little about electronics or stereos. I was surprised to be hired with my limited knowledge but accepted the job when it was offered. The manager of the store required that all employees come to work an hour early on Saturdays. I expected that we would be cleaning the store or restocking shelves. Surprisingly, that was not the purpose of the meeting. Instead, the manager taught us basic electronics.

In these Saturday morning classes I learned the details about tuners, amplifiers, and speakers that I needed to serve our customers well. After a couple of years I learned enough about electronics and store management that I was offered a position as manager of my own store.

Before I left for my new position, my manager took me to lunch to celebrate my promotion. I asked him why he had hired me in the first place given my lack of electronic knowledge. He told me, "Gary, I hired you because you have a good attitude. I can teach anyone about electronics, but I can't teach them to get along with people."

The principle of a culture of service is: *Recruit people for attitude, train people for skills.* Seek a balance between formal and informal training. Formal training works best when the ministry position is highly standardized. Provide training in a seminar format in short blocks of time. Many people are comfortable attending seminars or workshops for training in their business. Yet not all training needs to be formal. If someone in your church is excellent at providing care and service, put others with that person to learn informally.

Above all, repeatedly teach the mission, values, and philosophies that undergird your culture of service. People need to understand the whys and wherefores of your strategy. They need to be clear on your church's mission and how their ministry aids in its fulfillment. Don't assume your people know and understand these things; teach them.

Acknowledge and Reward

In every church I've attended there is a common ritual that takes place following a meal at the church. After the meal, the pastor stands up and asks for the cooks to come out of the kitchen so the people who have eaten can express their appreciation for the meal. Once the cooks and kitchen help have been coaxed out, the people applaud them. The moral of this story? People are motivated to do what they are rewarded for doing. So be sure you are rewarding for the results you want to see increased. If you want people to serve in any ministry, then acknowledge them for doing so.

The most popular way to motivate people is to reward them for service well done. I've heard of many creative ways to award people, but my favorite is the Golden Banana Award. One day at Hewlett-Packard, an employee burst into his manager's office with the solution to a problem the group had struggled with for weeks. Sensing the magnitude of the employee's contribution, the manager groped around his desk in a frantic search for something to give the employee to show his gratitude. Finally, he grabbed a banana from his lunch and handed it to the employee exclaiming, "Well done!" The Golden Banana Award became one of the company's most prestigious honors for inventiveness.

Serving people is hard, emotional labor, and it demands frequent bursts of extra effort. Awards give people the extra energy that keeps them serving with a smile. With a little thought I'm certain you can develop your own Golden Banana Award that will have meaning to your people. One church I visited handed out the Giant-Killer Award, named after the famous battle between David and Goliath. The essence of the award was to thank those who had faced the biggest challenge in ministry and won.

The best reward for service to others is a simple one—a handwritten memo of appreciation. At first thought, it might not sound like much of an award; but when people take the time to handwrite a letter or note, it means they really care.

Motivation, of course, comes from a positive culture or environment set in place by leadership. People who truly feel they are part of something important will desire to be vitally involved. The most powerful Golden Banana Award is the knowledge that they're following in the steps of Christ by serving others in a sacrificial way.

Everyone Serves

Ultimately, what a culture of service seeks is to empower everyone in the church to serve other people's needs. Tell people in your church that if they encounter another person with a need, they should try to find a solution to that need.

If they can't solve it, they should go to someone like their Sunday School teacher or small-group leader. If they can't solve the problem, they should take the problem to a pastor or committee chairperson or associate pastor. Then if *they* can't solve it, take it to the senior pastor (but take it to him last).

The idea is to allow people to minister to others. Everything doesn't need to be taken to the pastor or other church leaders. Give members permission to serve others by solving the problem themselves. They can do it if you'll give them permission and authority to do so.

Investing in People—A Summary

The Christians in Carthage, North Africa, in A.D. 252 are an excellent example of how God's people have always been willing to sacrificially serve others. They were called the "risk-takers" because of their courageous model.

♦   Leaders who desire to establish a culture of service in their church must take the most challenging risk of investing ministry in their people.

♦   The best way to empower people for service is to encourage and support their ideas for ministry. Leaders must learn to say yes to people's ideas for new ministries and help them get started.

+ There are essentially two ways to recruit people for service: institution-based recruiting and relation-based recruiting. In today's environment the best approach is to recruit people one by one using a personal interview system.

+ Training people takes place formally and informally. Formal training works best with highly standardized roles, and informal training works best for roles demanding lots of flexibility and creativity.

+ A way to motivate people is needed since most people tend to do what they are rewarded for doing. While there are numerous ways to reward people, the most appreciated one is a simple handwritten note of thanks.

―――

Something to Think About

Recruit people for attitude;
train people for skills.

―――

Look for Nice People

Take a few moments to list the qualifications you most often look for in people to serve in your church. ―――

――――――――――――――――――――――

――――――――――――――――――――――

――――――――――――――――――――――

To what degree do characteristics such as kindness, caring, compassion, and unselfishness show up on your list? ――――――――――――――――――――

――――――――――――――――――――――

――――――――――――――――――――――

――――――――――――――――――――――

To what degree do qualifications that reflect skills show up?_____

_____

_____

Are you recruiting for attitudes or for skills?_____

_____

_____

How is this reflected in your quality of service people inside and outside your church receive from your church?

_____

_____

_____

A System of Training

In most secular jobs I've held, training was always offered to help me initially learn and later improve my skills.

Unfortunately, I rarely received or was offered training when being asked to serve in a church ministry.

Read and answer the questions below about your system for training people in your church. It will take some effort but will be worthwhile.

1. What types of formal training do you offer people serving in your church to get started or improve their skills?

2. How many training events have you sponsored or sent your people to in the last year?

3. How much money is budgeted for training in your church this year?

4. When was the last time you held a training event specifically to remind people of your mission, values, and philosophy of ministry?

5. Do you have an award similar to the Golden Banana Award that is legendary in your church? Could you start one? What would you call it?

6. When was the last time you sent someone a handwritten note of thanks for a job well done?

7. Besides those who serve in your kitchen, who receives applause for faithful service, and how is it done?

What did you learn from these questions? What actions will you take? What can you do this week to get started?

Do it!

———

PART TWO

Preparing for a Culture of Service

CHAPTER FOUR

Get Ready for Company

*I*f you were to survey churches and ask them what their strengths are, almost everyone would include, "We're a friendly church." I know this for a fact as I have asked this question of more than five hundred churches since 1983 when I first began church consulting as a member of Win Arn's team at the Institute for American Church Growth.

In every church I surveyed, people either wrote on a survey or stated verbally that they believed their church to be friendly. It did not matter if they were attending churches in danger of closing down, in the midst of twenty-year-long plateaus, or bursting forth in growth. They all felt their churches were friendly. Being a friendly church apparently is a standard reply of all churches regardless of the reality of their growth or decline.

If you were to have surveyed the visitors who attended those same churches, however, you might have found the opposite perception. "Beauty is in the eye of the beholder." Let's adapt that truism: "Friendliness is in the eye of the beholder." Another way to say it is, "Perception is reality." We may think our church is friendly, but it is only friendly to the degree that those visiting our church perceive it to be so.

The Visitor's Perception

How is it that two people may experience the same event and yet feel so differently about it? Perception.

People who regularly attend a church look at the issue of friendliness from the inside out. From their perspective, they are experiencing a friendly atmosphere. They know other people, and other people know them. When they have a personal need, their friends take notice and respond with appropriate action. They perceive their church as a friendly place.

Visitors, in contrast, see the church from the outside in. From their perspective, they are experiencing a totally new atmosphere. They may not know other people, and other people may not know them. If they have needs, they are rarely noticed, let alone responded to with appropriate action. Their perception often sees the church as an unfriendly place.

Now we know that perception isn't always reality. For example, some people perceive that there is no God while in reality there is one. As Psalm 14:1 reminds us, "The fool has said in his heart, 'There is no God.'" In a similar way, it is possible for a church to be a friendly place and for some visitors to perceive otherwise. But this does not change the truth that in the "eye of the beholders"—in this case the visitors—perception will be their reality. The bottom line: If visitors do not perceive us as friendly, we are not.

My mother and grandmother were raised, committed themselves to the Lord, and attended church in Missouri and Oklahoma. They were loyal to church, like most people of their generation, attending every time the church doors opened. Then in 1947 after a fire destroyed their apartment in Tulsa, they moved to Colorado Springs to live closer to my uncle. They found jobs, rented a small house, and went looking for a church. Their experience was far from positive. They met unfriendly people in every church they attended. Their perception was that churches in Colorado Springs rejected them because of their Okie mannerisms. In reality, you and I know that every church they attended most likely was not that unfriendly. However, in the eyes of my mother and grandmother, the churches they visited were unfriendly, and that was reality as far as they were concerned. The perception was strong enough that my grandmother, who was fifty-one at the time, never attended any church on a regular basis the rest of her life—and she lived until she was ninety-eight!

The point is this: We must get ready for company! Company is coming to our church every Sunday, and what visitors perceive in our welcome will influence their feelings and response to church and the Lord for years to come. Their viewpoints and perceptions must be considered valuable. What are visitors perceiving about our church? How friendly do they perceive us to be? What steps can we take to welcome them better than we presently do?

Empty the Litter Boxes

Whenever company is coming over to our house my family goes through a regular ritual called "Getting Ready for Company." It involves such things as cleaning the bathrooms, emptying the trash, vacuuming the floor, dusting the counters, and, most important, changing the cat's litter boxes. We want our house to look its best, and we spare no effort to see that it is ready. No doubt you can identify with this experience.

Growing churches also spend a lot of time getting ready for their company—visitors—whom I prefer to call guests.

I suggest that we begin by eliminating the term *visitor* from our church vocabularies. In its place let us insert the term *guest*. Doing this is much more than some foolish policy of political correctness. Each term brings to mind different images, and how we imagine newcomers in our mind is how we will treat them.

If you were to visit me in California by showing up uninvited at my front door, I would answer your knock with a polite but awkward, "It's good to see you." Of course what I would really be thinking is, "What are you doing here?" I might even invite you inside, offer you a small snack, and graciously spend some time talking with you. Yet our time together would be somewhat strained since I didn't know you were coming and wasn't ready for you. After a brief visit, I would expect you to leave. As some people say, "Good food, good talk, good night!"

If I invited you to be my guest, however, things would be different. I would answer your knock with an enthusiastic, "Hi! I was expecting you to drop by." Once inside you would find that I had cleaned the house in preparation for your visit, and my wife had prepared your favorite meal. After an extended conversation, I would invite you to spend the night in our guest room. The next day as you started to leave, I would say, "It was a good time. Please come back soon."

Strategies for Building Church Self-Esteem

1. Be positive about yourself! Much of your church's self-esteem will depend on the tone you set as a leader. If you see the good in people, call it forth, bless it, and believe in it. They soon will begin to see themselves in the same light.

2. Celebrate the positives! Call attention to the good that happens to your church. . . . Celebrate high attendance and offerings. Make anniversaries a time to bless

the past and mark how far the church has come. Have a time for prayers of thankfulness that focus on the good God is doing in your church.

3. Change the language. Address problems as opportunities and challenges. Do not think of problems as limitations but as opportunities to be creative. Banish the word failure by blessing risk: "We are a church not afraid to try new things for God."

4. Change the rules. A pastor friend claimed the negative was three times more powerful than the positive, so he instituted a rule in every meeting: Three positive statements must be made before a negative comment could be offered.

5. Recruit cheerleaders! Find the people who have positive attitudes and believe in possibilities. Let them serve as cheerleaders by giving testimonies, taking leadership roles, and speaking out at decision-making times.

6. Recognize the heroes. Recognizing those who make a positive impact on the church sends a message that people are doing well and that your church is a good place.

7. Channel the negative. Some individuals try to project their own poor self-images on the church. Don't let them set the tone for the church. Channel their negative attitudes and comments in constructive ways.

—Adapted from Pastor Clay Smith, Southside Baptist Church
Louisville, Kentucky. See his article, "Seven Strategies for Building
Your Church's Self-Esteem" in *Growing Churches*,
(October/November/December 1993), 13.

What is the difference? In the first scenario you are a visitor; in the second you are a guest. Visitors are often unwanted; guests are expected. Visitors just show up; guests are invited. Visitors are expected to leave; guests are expected to stay. Visitors come one time; guests return again.

I used the term *visitor* in the opening sections of this book because that is the term with which we are most familiar. Yet in the rest of the book I will use the term *guest* so that we can begin to get into the habit of viewing newcomers to our church from a fresh perspective. I suggest you begin to change your vocabulary also. It will make a difference.

When You're the Host

Have you been a guest in someone's home and remembered it for years to come? The food was perfect, the friends were warm, and the music was relaxing. Or perhaps you attended a church where the time flew so quickly that you did not even want the service to end. It makes a difference when a visit to a home or a church is hosted well.

What does it take to be a good host and welcome our guests in a manner that will increase their desire to return? Whether our church is fifty people or five hundred or five thousand, we must attend to many responsibilities so that our guests feel welcomed. We must draw up a list and send out invitations. We must decide where people will park, how to direct them to the proper entrance, who will greet them as they arrive, and how to point out important locations such as the rest rooms. In addition, someone must determine where people will sit, what to prepare for refreshments, and what music is appropriate. The list of details can seem endless.

Getting ready for company requires us to think of ourselves as hosts and those who visit us as our guests. In scriptural terms, we must be hospitable. *Hospitality* literally means "love of strangers." In the New Testament this concept primarily refers to gracious acceptance and service toward fellow believers. Today we must not lose sight of the inherent implications toward outsiders. We can trace the concept of hospitality back to instructions given to the nation of Israel after they left Egypt. The Lord instructed the people of Israel, "When a stranger resides with you in your land, you shall not do him wrong. The stranger who resides with you shall be to you as the native among you, and you shall love him as yourself; for you were aliens in the land of Egypt; I am the LORD your God" (Lev. 19:33–34).

Four insights in these verses apply to welcoming strangers—our guests—to church. First, we are not to mistreat our guests in any way. Second, we are to treat them as one of our own. Third, we are to love them as we love ourselves. Fourth, why? Because we all were once strangers to church ourselves.

No Guests, No Growth

It seems too obvious to even mention, but sometimes the simple ideas are the ones we forget. So let us remind ourselves of two unmistakable facts:

1. It takes guests to grow. People do not become committed members of a church without first visiting the worship service and other ministries.

2. People no longer come to church simply because "it is the thing to do." Even when they do visit, well-worn methods of follow-up are not as effective as they once were in getting people to return, let alone become regular worshipers.

To understand some of the changes in welcoming guests, let us examine some percentages.

Sixty percent have little understanding of your church. In today's world only 40 percent of our guests will come from a sister church or one of a similar background. That means that 60 percent come with little or no understanding of our church. Just a little more than forty years ago approximately 90 percent of a church's guests came from the same denominational background. This meant that they already understood our church's theology, music, order of worship, values, and culture. Such inherent knowledge allowed them to feel comfortable and at ease in our church. We would have had little need to explain anything in a church of the 1950s.

Today with more than half of our guests coming with either no church background or from one that is quite different, it is a another story. There is a corresponding lack of knowledge about our church. Many guests will not be familiar with our worship format. They will not know when to stand, sit, or kneel. Others will not know our songs, language, and religious jargon.

Fifty percent fewer visitors per car than in the past. With the improvements in automobiles and roads following World War II, Americans grew even stronger in their love affair with the car. Families fitted the breadwinner-and-homemaker nuclear family format of father, mother, and 2.2 children. A pastor looking out his office window in the early 1950s would have counted three or four people in every car driving into the church parking lot.

A pastor viewing cars out the same window today will most often see only one or two people in each car. Today each family unit is about half the size and each car brings about 50 percent fewer people to church. Each guest arriving at our church is more valuable in the sense that fewer are visiting. We must be more effective in welcoming those who do take the initiative to visit.

Ten percent of church members leave each year. People stayed longer in churches of the early 1950s. The best guess is that in those times churches lost only about 5 percent of their people each year. Family units were still intact, neighborhoods and mutual networks of friendships were fairly strong. The general culture supported a friendliness that benefited churches with a natural openness, providing a friendly welcome to all who came. This, coupled with the tendency of people to remain in the same geographical area and with the same job for a lifetime, made concerns for welcoming guests less of an issue.

Today churches lose about 10 percent of their worshipers a year (some much more). Our mobile society finds people moving three to six times, with some moving up to twenty times, in a lifetime. Add to this the fracturing of the family and the breakdown of natural networks of friendships and we can see that it is more of a challenge to welcome guests today.

Sixteen percent of guests need to stay. Research completed in the late 1980s found that a church must keep about 16 percent of its first-time guests in order to experience a minimal growth rate of 5 percent a year. Rapidly growing churches keep about 25 to 30 percent of their first-time guests. Declining churches keep only about 5 to 8 percent of their first-time guests. By using the average of 16 percent, we can calculate how many guests our church needs to grow. As an example, a church that wants to add fifty new members this year will need to have at least three hundred guests attend its worship services during the year.

Eighty-five percent of visitors who return the next Sunday stay. The same research revealed the crucial importance of getting guests to return for a second visit. A church keeps about 85 percent of its guests who come back the next week for a second visit. This points out the importance of being gracious hosts the first time so that our guests will feel encouraged to return again.

Instinctively we expect churches to be friendly places. Research studies completed by Win Arn in the mid-1980s found direct correlation between friendliness and potential growth. Arn found that friendly churches had great potential for growth while less friendly churches had little potential for growth.[1] Let's get ready for company!

Welcoming Guests—A Summary

♦   All churches believe they are friendly. However, friendli-
    ness is in the eye of the beholder—depending on
    whether it is viewed from the inside or the outside.

♦   Terms create powerful images. Getting ready for com-
    pany means we must develop a new example which
    views newcomers to our church as guests rather than
    visitors.

♦   Hospitality means "love of strangers." There are four key
    insights on welcoming strangers—guests—to our
    church.

> 1. Do not mistreat guests in any way.
>
> 2. Treat guests as one of our own church family.
>
> 3. Love guests as we love ourselves.
>
> 4. Remember: We were once strangers to the family
>   of God.

♦   Without guests a church cannot grow. Our changing
    world has created a need to be more intentional in
    welcoming guests to our church.

    —60 percent of our guests will not have the background
    to understand our church without our assistance.
    —50 percent fewer people are coming per car and in
    each family unit.
    —10 percent of a church's worshipers leave every year
    (some more), who will need to be replaced to stay even
    or increased to grow.
    —16 percent of first-time guests continuing on in regular
    attendance is a minimal number for our church to grow.
    —85 percent of the people who return for a second visit
    will likely continue on as regular worshipers in our
    church.

♦ The Exodus Principle is a manual to consult time and time again for ideas on how to welcome guests to our church.

———

Something to Think About

If guests to our church don't think we're friendly, we aren't.

———

Seven Ways to Be a Good Host

1. Invite our guests with a personal invitation.
2. Arrive early to make sure everything is ready for our guests' arrival.
3. Greet our guests warmly at the entrance and escort them to their seats.
4. Assist guests in understanding what is taking place.
5. Anticipate and answer as many questions as possible in advance so guests do not have to ask.
6. Do something extra to make guests' visit special.
7. Walk guests to the door and invite them back.

Assessing Your Skills as a Host

Want to have a productive day? Take a legal pad, sit down for an hour, and work your way through each of the "Seven Ways to Be a Good Host."

Write each statement by number leaving five to ten lines under each one. Make a list under each one, noting every way your church presently accomplishes that aspect of being a good host to your guests. When you are finished, go back with a different color of pen and generate a second list of new ways to fulfill each area.

Once you've completed this on your own, consider working through the list with appropriate boards or committees in your church. Simply write each statement on a chalkboard and list ideas beneath.

You will not only assess your current success of being a good host, but you will challenge yourself to being even better in the days ahead.

———

CHAPTER FIVE

Develop Guest Eyes

*U*pon visiting a church in Indiana, I walked into the church lobby, and the person with me commented, "You will like our church. It's a very friendly place." Once inside the building, we were immediately met by a man carrying an armful of papers. Introductions were polite, and we shook hands. It was what followed that surprised me, however.

Upon completing our handshake, the man turned to my friend and began to talk about some church business that should not have been discussed in my presence.

As they talked, the man moved nervously back and forth on his feet, gradually shifting his position. Within a few minutes his back was actually pointed toward me.

I remember thinking to myself, *Hey! I'm the guest here. Quit ignoring me!* Yet I didn't say anything to him.

When he had finished discussing his bit of church business, he seemed to catch a glimpse of me out of the side of his eye. In an embarrassed and hasty attempt to make me feel welcome, he turned toward me and said, "It was nice to meet you. You'll like our church. It's a very friendly place."

Important Facts about Church Guests

When a person talks to a member of our church, or calls on the telephone, or receives a brochure in the mail, or drives into our parking lot, or whatever, it is a moment of truth.

A *moment of truth* (MOT) is any occasion in which a person comes into contact with, and forms an impression of, our church. Admittedly, it is hard to evaluate the success or quality of these moments of truth. There is little tangible evidence to evaluate. That is why it is so hard to assess the effectiveness of such encounters. The end result of a moment of truth in the life of a guest is a feeling about our church—good or bad. We want it to be a good feeling.

Before we consider how to describe, analyze, and assess the quality of our guests' experience with the critical moments of truth, we need to understand four important facts.

People Seldom Think about Our Church

People outside of our church do not go around thinking about us. Those of us who are church leaders tend to be consumed constantly with the concerns of our church. There may be hardly an hour that goes by without some thought concerning our church. In many cases we extend our burden for our church to others, thinking unconsciously that others know about and think about our church also.

Wake up! This is not the case. People outside of our church are bombarded with so much daily information that they probably have never thought of our church—not even once.

I was shocked into this reality while pastoring a church in San Bernardino, California. In an effort to greet people and introduce them to our church, we organized a neighborhood canvass. Sixteen of our leaders went door-to-door talking to people and telling them about the ministry of our church. Following each two-hour time period, we would meet back at the church to discuss our experiences. During one such discussion, one of our elders reported about a neighbor who had asked where our church was located, mentioning that she had never seen the building. He kindly pointed out our building, which could be seen just down her street. This woman had lived in her home for ten years, and our church had been on the same street for nearly twenty-three years. She had lived only two blocks from our church and didn't know we were there!

Now she obviously had driven past our church during those ten years. The issue was not had she ever seen us, for she clearly could not have missed us. The issue was that she never *thought* of us. We were never on her mind! It is the opposite of the old saying, "Out of sight; out of mind." For people in our information-saturated society, it reads, "Out of mind; out of sight." Since she did not think of us, she never saw us, even when we were right down the block.

People Think of Us Only When They Contact Us

Remember that our church only exists in such a person's mind when he or she makes some type of contact with us, either directly or indirectly.

The woman who lived just down the street from our church knew nothing about our ministries, our people, our child care, or our worship service. Even the visible picture of our building, landscaping, and sign were not developed in her mind. She did, however, come face-to-face with our church in that moment of truth when an elder talked with her in her yard. In that instant she met our church and made some important evaluations about our leadership and ministry.

I am unaware of any studies of the number of impressions made during moments of truth in relationship to a church.

However, one secular report notes that people, on the average, make eleven decisions about us in the first seven seconds of contact.[1] There is no doubt that the woman living just down the street from our church was making quick evaluations about our church. Impressions that would last for years in her mind. Let's not underestimate these moments of truth.

People Extend Their First Impression to Our Entire Church

Here is a sobering fact: People outside of our church extend their impressions from brief moments of truth to cover our entire church.

Three years ago I was board chairman of a local Christian high school that wanted to relocate to a better facility. One day while driving in the north end of town, I went past a Baptist church that was where we had hoped to relocate. The church buildings appeared large enough to accommodate our school, but what caught my eye in that moment of truth was the number of tall weeds growing out of cracks in the parking lot. Upon further investigation I found all the gates and fences locked. Although I couldn't see through the stained glass windows, the building appeared to be deserted. I immediately made my eleven decisions about that church—the most exciting of which was that the church must be closed and possibly for sale. Once I arrived home I began making phone calls attempting to track down someone with information about this church. Eventually, I received a return phone call. I introduced myself and explained that I had noticed the run-down building and wondered if it was for sale. My bluntness must have shocked the person, for his response was a classic case of "the silence was deafening." In no uncertain terms he corrected my impressions by informing me that the church was open and not for sale. He asked, "How could you have come to such an illogical conclusion?"

That's easy to explain. I simply generalized my impressions from one single moment of truth to the entire church.

The sad aspect of this encounter was not that the building was unavailable to my Christian school. More crucial was the probability that many people came to the same conclusions I did and drove right on by without visiting.

People's Contact Results in a Feeling about Our Church

Think back to the opening story of this chapter. What do you think I felt about the church I visited in Indiana? As I recall, the worship service was excellent. The Sunday School class I attended kept my attention and several people greeted me. The church buildings were new, clean, and invitingly up-to-date. Yet, everytime I think about that particular church, I remember that first moment of truth in the foyer.

In this case my feeling was neither positive nor negative, which may be worse. Being an experienced church visitor, I am not going to write the church off as unfriendly. Yet I do not carry a strong positive feeling about the church simply because of that one moment of truth.

Consider the woman down the street from the church I pastored. What do you think she felt about our church after meeting one of our elders? It's hard to know, isn't it? But whatever she felt in that moment of truth became her impression of our entire church.

The Gardening Process

Close your eyes and envision in your mind a beautiful garden. If you are like me, you do not picture a single flower or plant but an entire garden in full bloom. If an image is not forming clearly, simply picture a single rose. Then, picture a dozen roses in a beautiful vase. Finally, picture an entire garden of roses. Which picture makes the greatest impact? The single rose, or the dozen roses, or the rose garden?

It depends. At times nothing outshines a display of a dozen roses. The bouquet created with the roses, baby's breath, and vase is beautiful. At other times, the gift of a single rose will melt the heart of someone you love. Still, the cumulative effect of an entire rose garden is magnificent.

I'm a pastor accustomed to greeting people in church, but this Sunday morning my wife and I were away from home. A week of isolation for rest and study made us ready for worship and fellowship. When we entered the church, people were standing in small circles talking with their friends. Nobody paid any attention to us.

As we stood in the middle of the room, I caught the eye of a man my age, but he was too engrossed in conversation to reach out to someone he didn't know. At last an older woman came and introduced herself, brought us coffee, and introduced us to her husband and then another couple.

When the group broke up, we followed upstairs to the chapel, which was nearly full. Someone gave us a bulletin, but no one showed us where to sit. The only vacant seats were down in front, and we were afraid they might be saved.

We stood there, feeling awkward for what seemed like a long time, but again we were rescued by the woman who had brought us coffee. She ushered us down the aisle and asked some people to move over to make room for us.

One person made a significant difference. It has been months since we visited that church. I remember the pastor was evangelical, but I don't remember a thing he said. I do remember the people who didn't have time for us and the one woman and her husband who did. That *experience made me appreciate ushers and greeters and people in churches who make extraordinary efforts to reach out and welcome newcomers. The biblical call to "Welcome each other . . . just as Christ has warmly welcomed you" (Rom. 15:7, TLB) is an important message to every new person who comes to church.*

—Donald Bubna, "How Well Do You Say Welcome?"
Moody, March 1988, 18–19.

Such is the possibility of the moments of truth encountered by people outside our church. A single encounter may be engaging, but in most situations the cumulative effect of several moments of truth form the most powerful impact. My moment of truth driving by the church with weeds growing in the parking lot was like a single rose. That one impression impacted my view of the church significantly.

My experience with the church in Indianapolis was like a dozen roses displayed in a vase. The numerous moments of truth formed a better picture of the church which, together, lessened the negative impact of the first encounter. What I did not experience at that church, of course, was a total perception which could only have come by observing their entire garden of moments of truth.

Eleven Moments of Truth

Thinking of a church in terms of moments of truth is a powerful tool to help us address and evaluate the quality of our friendliness. It enables us to redirect our thinking away from tedious programs to exciting service of those Christ has called us to reach.

By defining the moments of truth likely to be encountered by guests to our church, we can begin to build a church that is indeed friendly and inviting to those outside the church.

There are, of course, many moments of truth. However, standard ones are met by guests to every church. Read through each one and think what happens now and what should happen when a guest encounters each moment of truth at our church.

MOT 1: Receiving an Invitation to Church

Not many people visit a church today without receiving some form of invitation. It may come through a personal contact with a friend at work or next door, or it may be a direct mail piece sent to the home.

It's true: "You do not have a second chance to make a first impression." First impressions impact us more than any other single moment of truth, though they may be overpowered by the total perception created by several moments of truth.

MOT 2: Driving by the Church Building

For some, this second moment of truth will be their first impression. If our church is located in a high traffic area, we can be certain that many people are driving by each day. For others, when they drive up to the facility, an additional moment of truth is added to other previous encounters.

Among other aspects, they will notice if the landscaping around our church is well kept; if the parking lot is nicely paved and clear of debris; and if there are parking spaces clearly marked for guests.

MOT 3: Walking to the Front Door

Getting out of their car and walking to the church building is a major moment of truth for most guests. Some start to feel tense as they imagine what they will find inside. Will there be warm and friendly people? Are they entering through the proper door? Will they need to ask a lot of embarrassing questions? Are they dressed appropriately?

MOT 4: Entering the Front Door

New guests form most of their impressions about a church during the first thirty seconds of walking in the front door. All their feelings are subconscious, but they are being made quickly nonetheless. Contributing to their subconscious thoughts are such items as sounds, smells, signs, pictures, bulletin boards, colors, lighting, and the general decor.

MOT 5: Meeting People

Initial contacts with people play a major role in the thoughts of guests toward a church. Are church members outgoing and approachable? Do they express an attitude of acceptance? Is there an honest friendliness without being mushy or overbearing? Are there friendly people available to answer questions and give assistance? Much of the impact made on guests comes through the body language of people they meet. Simple actions such as smiling or frowning leave lasting images on a new guest.

MOT 6: Experiencing Ministries and Services

The ministries or amenities explored will vary from guest to guest. Those with small children want to find a child care area that is clean, bright, open, and safe. Those needing to use the rest rooms hope to find them clean and free of unpleasant odors. Those attending a class expect comfortable and well-decorated classrooms staffed with gracious people.

MOT 7: Entering the Sanctuary

Guests entering the worship area wish to find smiling ushers exhibiting a servant attitude. The atmosphere of the worship service is expected to be vibrant and happy. Guests expect to find room to sit without being crowded. They want to be welcomed graciously and treated with respect.

MOT 8: Participating in the Worship Service

As guests, they may not know our church's tradition or practice in worship. They hope to find an easy way to understand and follow the order of worship. They may hope to hear songs that are familiar and easy to learn, or they may prefer to be left alone to listen to the music without being forced to participate. Most guests hope to feel at ease and comfortable. They pray that our worship service will not go too long.

MOT 9: Exiting the Worship Service

Guests trust that upon leaving the worship area they will find a friendly atmosphere where they are greeted but not attacked. Most are open to invitations to a refreshment table to talk and meet others. Yet they want to feel that they have a choice in staying or leaving—no arm twisting, please.

MOT 10: Contacting People the First Week

Most guests do not want an unannounced visit to their home. Yet they are more than ready to talk by phone and share their personal feelings about their visit to our church. They appreciate a gracious invitation to return, as well as a personal letter from the pastor.

MOT 11: Contacts in the Months Ahead

Guests expect to end up on our mailing list to receive appropriate information in the months ahead. Most people appreciate a church newsletter, informational brochures describing ministries they might find interesting, and occasional personal invitations to special events.

An interesting factor comes into play in Olympic events such as figure skating and gymnastics. All aspects of the performance count in the final score, but the most crucial factors are the beginning and the end. If an Olympic athlete begins well and ends well, then all's well. The implication is that the first and last impressions are the most important on the final score.

These words of wisdom fit moments of truth as well. The most important moments of truth for guests are their first and last ones. Guests have already made many judgments about our church before our pastor even stands up to preach. Impressions that are formed by the first moment of truth are carried along, affecting, to some degree, all succeeding encounters. Since the last moment of truth remains freshest in the mind, it is stronger than those that fall in between. The total perception comes into play, but be certain that the first and last moments of truth are extremely powerful.

Seasons of Service

Fourth Season
◆ Future mailings
◆ Future invitations
◆ Future visits
◆ Future ministry

First Season
◆ Initial invitations
◆ Contact with members
◆ Drive-by facilities
◆ Advertising received

MOT # 1

Other MOTS — MOT # 2

Moments
of
Truth

MOT # 11 — MOTS # 3 & 4

MOT # 10 — MOTS # 5-8

MOT # 9

Third Season
◆ Refreshments
◆ Invitation to return
◆ Follow-up

Second Season
◆ First visit to church
◆ First worship service
◆ First ministry participation

Some people will experience a moment of truth independently apart from others. Yet those who come into contact with a church several times will discover a complete sequence of moments. Ultimately, their impression will be formed from a garden of experiences rather than a single event. The moments of truth already listed form a regular "season of service" through which we may trace the path of our guests and evaluate our service to them (see illustration on p. 81).

What do guests see, experience, and feel from these moments of truth in our church? What should they have experienced? What can our church begin to do to make these moments of truth positive experiences for our guests?

Forming Impressions—A Summary

♦ A moment of truth (MOT) is any occasion in which a person comes into contact with, and forms an impression of, our church.

♦ Four concepts foundational to understanding the power of MOTS:

1. People outside our church do not go around thinking about us.

2. People only think about our church when they come into direct or indirect contact with us.

3. People tend to generalize their experience from a single MOT to our entire church.

4. People leave their MOT encounter with a positive or negative feeling about our church.

♦ The accumulated impact of several MOTS is more powerful than a single one.

♦ The first and last MOTS experienced by guests tend to define their entire impression of our church.

- There are many potential MOTS, but there are predictable seasons through which church guests will travel.

―――

Something to Think About

Guests form most of their opinions about our church within thirty seconds of entering the front door.

―――

Think Like a Guest

If you were a guest visiting our church . . .

1. Would you be impressed by the facility and landscaping?
2. Would you be able to find the rest rooms without asking?
3. Would you feel comfortable leaving your child in the nursery?
4. Would you understand what takes place during the worship service?
5. Would you be embarrassed or pressured during your visit?
6. Would you be greeted and accepted as you are?
7. Would you come back next week?

Developing Guest Eyes

To honestly appreciate the new person's experience, you need to set aside your "insider" understanding about your church and think like an "outsider." A good way to do so is to walk through the key moments of truth that guests to your church encounter.

Do you want to have an extra special and fruitful board meeting? Then try the following.

- Start by making up copies of the moments of truth discussed in this chapter. All you need to do is type out

the headings leaving two to three inches of space beneath each one.

♦ At your next board meeting, ask each member to leave
  everything in the boardroom except a pen or pencil and
  walk with you about a block away from your church.

♦ Then explain that you want them to pretend they have
  never been to your church before. Tell them to look at
  your church through "guest eyes" and jot down what
  guests see as they encounter each moment of truth listed
  on the paper you hand out to them.

♦ Next, actually walk through the moments of truth, stopping briefly at each area to allow your leaders to look
  around and write down what guests see.

♦ Complete your tour back in your boardroom and debrief
  the experience, going through the moments of truth
  from beginning to end. _____

CHAPTER SIX

Upgrade Your Ministries

W arm, fuzzy thoughts usually come to mind when we begin to think of a culture of service—things like smiling and being polite. Positive attitudes and actions are a necessary part of a growing church. We can smile all we want, but if people do not find they are being served well through our various ministries, they aren't likely to return anytime soon. Even more crucial: if our regular worshipers don't have pride in our church and ministry, they won't bring their friends.

I observed the Pride Factor in action a few years ago when my wife and I decided to have our driveway enlarged. The company we hired to do the job was owned and operated by two brothers who were both Christians and committed church members. We had developed a friendship and talked quite a bit while the work was in progress.

One day we were engaged in casual conversation when one of the brothers asked me if I knew of a good church where he could take a close friend. His question shocked me since

I knew he attended a church in our city. Picking up on my surprised expression, he launched into a discourse about how he loved his present church, his pastor, and the people he had known there for many years. He was hesitant though about inviting his close friend, who was not a Christian, to attend his church.

Continuing on, he commented that he worshiped at his church because his old friends were there, but he was afraid to bring any new friends. He knew that his church's facilities, ministries, and, specifically, the worship service did not have the qualities that attracted newcomers. Quietly he whispered that if he was looking for a new church he probably wouldn't even attend his present church. His Pride Factor was low, and it prevented him from bringing his friend to worship there. Is church growth an extension of happy people? Yes, to some extent. People won't bring their friends to church if they're not happy at their church.

Rising Expectations

Anyone who has been around churches for many years realizes that people have higher expectations today than they did years ago. This is true in all areas of our lives. Demographic factors have played an important role in raising our expectations. One demographer observes,

> The quality of people who serve is fast becoming the critical factor in business competition. This is because the enormous baby-boom generation is beginning to make money. Households headed by 35-to-50-year-olds will control 42 percent of household income by 2000. More than half of these households will have incomes of $35,000 and over (in 1985 dollars). They will demand good service, and they will be able to pay for it. If they don't get it from your company, they'll get it from your competitor.[1]

A good example of rising expectations can be seen in what today's parents expect from the child care ministry of a church. Child care always has been a contributing factor in growing churches. Parents are naturally concerned for their children and want to place them in capable hands while they participate in church activities. Our changing lifestyle, however has meant that child care has taken on a major emphasis in our society. In the past couple of years I've noticed that bowling alleys and shopping centers provide child care for their customers.

While parents throughout history have loved and cared for their children, today's parents approach child care with higher expectations than those of only twenty years ago. About one-sixth of today's parents are over the age of thirty. Older parents expect more from your child care ministry than younger parents. These same parents are spending greater amounts of money on their children than parents used to spend.

Since 1980, Americans have increased their spending for infant and toddler clothing by 120 percent, according to the U.S. Bureau of Labor Statistics. With fewer children at home, parents not only want the best for their children but they are willing to spend the big bucks to get it. Nike, Chanel, Ralph Lauren, Christian Dior, and Guess? are among the many big-name designers who have introduced infant or toddler clothes.

Parents expect your church to be willing to spend money to provide the best for their children. It is not unusual for today's parents to spend $1,000 decorating a baby's room and more than $300 to furnish it with toys. Parents accordingly expect your church's nursery to be comparable to their baby's room at home. Parents who bring their children to your church are experienced child care shoppers. Many parents hire people to take care of their children during the workday. Whether they place their children in day care centers or with in-home care providers, they are experienced at shopping for quality care. Parents expect your church to provide the same quality care they would find at the best day care centers.

A Notch Above

Developing a culture of service is difficult when the core ministries and facilities of a church are below the standards or expectations of the people you are attempting to reach. One church I consulted with was located in a very hot climate. Most people in the city had air-conditioning in their homes, cars, and workplace. If they attended a movie, ate at a restaurant, or visited a doctor's office, they did it all in air-conditioned comfort. Yet the church was not air-conditioned! The members couldn't see the necessity of spending the money to air-condition their building.

If their church had developed a culture of service, they would have known that providing air-conditioning is a way of serving those they were trying to reach with the gospel. The high cost of installing central air-conditioning was part of their sacrificial service to people not yet a part of their church.

As a rule of thumb, your church's ministries and facilities need to be a "notch above" what your constituency expects or even needs. There are always exceptions, but most people lean toward attending a church that is slightly above their socioeconomic position in life. This means that if people live, work, and play in air-conditioning, they not only expect your church to be air-conditioned, but they expect it to be a notch better than theirs. Parents don't want your child care to be as good as theirs at home—they want it a notch above that. Those with super sound systems in their cars and homes will expect your church's sound system to be excellent. Thus, it is vitally important to upgrade your ministries as much as feasible to enhance the overall service level of your church.

Core Ministries

Serving people inside and outside of your church means upgrading your church as much as possible in all areas of ministry. You will want to begin by focusing on three core ministries: facilities, child care, and worship. A study conducted of those who do not attend church asked the question, "If you were to attend church, what would you look for?" The two main answers were a worship service that doesn't bore and excellent child care. Both of these two ministries must be housed in a facility that adds to their excellence.

Facility

Why worry about your facilities and grounds? Because you are developing an atmosphere for your church. How we decorate and present our facilities tells people a lot about our church and our values. It also sends a hidden message that we care and are interested in serving those whom God directs our way. The inherent message from well-designed, decorated, and kept facilities says, "We care about our church and we care about you."

Periodically look at your grounds, buildings, and facilities and ask, "Is there anything we need to change?" Look at it as a visitor would. Does it look inviting? Is it done in good taste? Should the carpet be replaced? Is there anything that looks out of date? Is there anything that would cause people to say, "I like that"? You want people to feel a sort of "wow" factor when they drive up or walk into your church building. The furniture, fixtures, lights—every detail—should contribute to making people's visit to your church a pleasant experience. People should walk in and say, "Oh," rather than, "Ouch."

Decor. I suggest you watch carefully the overall image your church communicates through its colors, style, and decorations to those who visit. I was asked to visit a church in California that once had been a model for other churches in the Southwestern part of the United States. Walking into the sanctuary, a bygone era screamed out to me through the colors (paint and carpet), styles (drapes and furniture), and displays (pictures and literature tables).

While observing another church, I noted a musty odor immediately upon entering the building. My recommendation to the church leaders of both churches was to hire a professional to advise them on how they could update the atmosphere of their sanctuary. For one church it simply meant removing twenty-five-year-old carpet and installing new padding and carpet to rid its building of a damp, musty smell that had accumulated over the years.

The other church faced more extensive remodeling that would take place over a period of three to five years. Understandably most churches cannot afford to replace furniture and make structural changes to their facilities very often. The expense is prohibitive. Churches ought to, however, plan on redecorating every five years by replacing or upgrading paint, landscaping, signs, fixtures, drapes, and other decorative items that can be changed fairly easily.

Clean Rest Rooms. Making sure the rest rooms are immaculate and tastefully decorated is an important way to show people that we care.

The huge education building gave evidence of what used to be a large and vibrant Sunday School program. Now, as the pastor led me on a tour of the church buildings, he was lamenting the lack of attendance and asking questions beginning with the word why. I made a list of items to discuss later, noting the narrow hallways, which had been painted purple and the dark brown carpet, but what really caused me distress were the rest rooms.

One women's rest room had a lightbulb hanging down about one foot from the ceiling by an electrical cord. In another there was no mirror. In yet another, the stench was so bad that I wouldn't want to use it. After my direct assessment of the rest rooms, the church board immediately appropriated the money to remodel the women's rest rooms. I had the opportunity to see a newly remodeled one about six months later. The new carpet, fixtures, lighting, mirrors, and chairs were very attractive and inviting. The rest room made a new statement to those who used it. It now said, "We care about you and are here to serve you." What a difference from the previous statement.

Directional Signs. Signs are a system for telling people how to get into our building and to wherever they hope to go. Most people would rather read a sign that points to the rest rooms than to ask for directions.

Arriving at a church in New Jersey, I parked two blocks away and walked in snow and ice to the front of the building where I was to preach. The sign said "Sanctuary" and pointed to what was obviously the front door. Rushing up the steps, I opened the door, walked through a dark entryway, and entered a second door to embarrassingly find myself standing at the front of the sanctuary with the entire congregation staring directly at me. Later, the pastor explained that the entrance I used was the front entrance many years before. A remodeling of the building had resulted in the complete reversal of the sanctuary. Now everyone entered through what at one time was the back entrance. There was only one small problem—they hadn't changed the sign! Everyone who attended the church regularly just knew to enter the back door, not the front door. I wondered how many guests had made the same mistake as I did. I didn't need to wonder how they felt. I already knew.

There are only three reasons for a sign: to name your church, to describe your services, and to give directions. If a sign doesn't do one of these three things, take it down. It's useless. Like other aspects of your facilities, signs communicate your values in a subtle way. So, do them right. Make sure signs match. Colors, logos, pictures, and, of course, the directions on them should be up-to-date and correct.

Child Care

Things change, and so must the carpet, designs, colors, furniture, and decorations. One place that must be clean and up-to-date is your child care rooms—parents notice! Sanitize your child care areas weekly. Regularly clean all surfaces, toys, tables, trays, bedding, bibs, and doors. Place used toys in a bin marked for washing and clean them each week. Clean carpets every other month. Clean walls every month. Redecorate every year. Cute animals are always in style. One year it might be dinosaurs, another year ducks.

Evaluate the ratio of children to nursery workers. With trained child care professionals, there should be no more than four infants per worker, and no more than five toddlers per worker. If you use volunteer workers, it is best if there are just two infants or four toddlers per worker. Provide a hazard-free environment. Replace broken toys, books, and furniture. Fix peeling paint, protruding nails, leaking plumbing, and lighting problems. Separate toddlers from babies. Use fire alarms and check them on a regular basis. Maintain good ventilation, heating, and air-conditioning.

Develop child care policies. Policies should contain information on how discipline is handled, procedures in case of sickness or accident, age guidelines, hours of operation, wellness policies, use of volunteers, registration procedures, and a fire escape plan. Provide a copy for all parents and post one near the entrance of all child care rooms.

As in most other roles, parents like to see the same people in the nursery and other child care ministries to gain a sense of trust. A high turnover rate of workers keeps children and parents from building relationships. Rotate workers as little as possible.

Train all child care workers. Explain to them how they are a vital link in your culture of service and how they fit into the overall philosophy of your church. Require workers to take first aid training and CPR for infants and children. Recruit and hire workers who interact well with children. It's even wise to screen all child care personnel for past history of child abuse.

Worship

Four distinct worship styles are popular in the United States today. Some churches enjoy a high church or Episcopal style where rituals, formal readings, and church architecture present people with a picture of the majesty of God. Others appreciate a less formal but traditional style, which maintains a respect for God through its hymns, prayers, and quiet atmosphere. A more contemporary worship style is gaining rapid acceptance today. People like the celebrative atmosphere that allows for personal interaction and the use of new technology and forms of communication, like drama. Lastly, many people find that a charismatic style of worship allows them to freely express and communicate their relationship to God in a joyous manner.

Remember that your message is not the sermon: your message is the service. Your entire worship service, from beginning to end, is sending a message. Excellent worship services send out a unified message by building the entire worship service around one theme. Once a broad theme has been selected, then each aspect of the service—music, introductions, announcements, Scripture reading, prayers, drama, sermon—are selected to support the theme.

Design your worship service to keep people alert by involving them in meaningful ways throughout the service. Build in ways for people to participate by allowing for singing, clapping, standing, shaking hands, praying, hugging, talking, laughing, crying, and other ways that would be acceptable to your worshipers.

Pay attention to the flow of the service. Once people enter into the worship time, the service should flow with good pace from one element to the next. While there is no need to rush the service, it needs to move along quickly enough to keep people's attention focused. Worshipers should be able to sense a clear flow or progression in the service. A sense of flow and pace happens when there is little "dead time" or few spots where nothing significant takes place in the service.

Good transitions between the elements of the worship service is a key aspect to develop in this respect. Incorporating a variety of worship elements—drama, interviews, video, a message, a greeting, Scripture reading, offering, and music—maintains everyone's interest and enjoyment.

Your Worship Service Is Celebrative When . . .

1. People attend. Celebrative services attract people who come because they want to rather than because they have to.

2. People bring friends. Celebrative services not only attract people, but they also cause worshipers to bring their friends.

3. People participate. Celebrative services create an environment where singing, giving, praying, and other areas of worship are entered into with enthusiasm.

4. People listen. Celebrative services hold the attention of worshipers throughout the entire time of worship.

5. People grow. Celebrative services challenge individuals to make biblical decisions that affect their daily living.

—From *The Issachar Factor* by Glen Martin and Gary McIntosh
(Nashville: Broadman & Holman Publishers, 1993)

To develop this type of worship service requires advance planning. It also helps to recruit a creative worship team to plan your services. Above all, effective worship services take seriously the mental, spiritual, relational, and emotional nature of the worshipers. Although the service should challenge worshiper's minds, it must also speak to the emotions, spirits, and hearts of the worshipers to be truly celebrative.

Little Changes Go a Long Way

It doesn't always take major changes to upgrade your ministries. A few changes can make dramatic improvements. You can't make big changes all the time, but you can make small improvements and make them continuously.

Pat Riley, former coach of the Los Angeles Lakers used the strategy of small improvements and saw the Lakers repeat as world champions. Intuitively he knew that the other NBA teams would be improving their game during the off season. If the Lakers didn't improve during the off-season, they would have little opportunity to be champions the following year. He challenged each player to improve just 1 percent in each of five areas during the next season. The five areas varied between each player according to his position and predominant skills.

Coach Riley knew that if they improved only 1 percent in five different areas they each would raise the level of their game 5 percent. That would mean the entire team of twelve players combined would improve their game 60 percent! His theory worked, and the Lakers repeated as champions.

World champion teams that don't improve rarely repeat for a second, third, or fourth year. The same is true of our church ministry. If we don't see small improvements taking place regularly, the quality of our ministries may be heading downward. We don't have to see major improvements all at once. Our challenge is to make little changes, incremental improvements each and every year. Raising the quality of twelve key ministries by only 1 percent each amounts to about a 12 percent increase in a year. Doing that for five years in a row would result in a 60 percent improvement.

Improving Your Ministries—A Summary

♦ The Pride Factor determines the willingness of your worshipers to bring new people to church. If they feel good about your church and the ministry it provides, they are more likely to bring their friends and family members to church. While they may attend your church themselves, if they are embarrassed by your ministries they are unlikely to risk bringing others.

♦ People expect churches to provide a higher quality of ministry today than they did in the past. An example of these higher expectations may be seen in the parents who bring their children to church today.

♦ As a rule of thumb, people worship at a church that offers a quality of ministry and a facility that is a notch above their socioeconomic standing.

♦ Grounds and facilities need to be redecorated every three to five years so that guests attending your church don't feel you are out-of-date.

♦ Worship services should be designed to present a unified message to the entire congregation.

Something to Think About

*The quality of your church buildings, grounds, and ministries
sends a message to people.
What message is being sent by your church?*

Visit Your Nursery

Take a tour of your church nursery as if you were a parent leaving your child there for the first time.

1. Would you be impressed with the decorations and furnishings?_____

2. Would you be pleased with the cleanliness of the carpet, walls, cribs, and toys?_____

3. Would you find the child care policies and fire escape plan posted for easy reading?_____

4. Would there be anything that would make you hesitate or feel uncomfortable about leaving your child there?

_____

5. Would you sense that your church has taken steps to insure the safety and welfare of your child?_____

   After your tour of the nursery, make a list of what can be done to serve your people better in the next year.

Twelve Key Ministries

Evaluate all your current ministries and make a list of the twelve more important ones to your church and its future.

   Looking over your list, what could you do this year in each area to improve it by only 1 percent? How could you upgrade each area this year so that it will be better next year? Be as specific and practical as possible.

   Once you've made your list, get started. If you accomplish each task, you'll have upgraded your ministries about 12 percent.

   Plan your upgrades over three to five years. For example, you may need a new sound system in the sanctuary. If you are unable to purchase the entire system this year, at least buy new microphones. Next year,

purchase the speakers and so on. By doing this for five
years you will eventually have your new sound system.

———

PART THREE

Communicating a Culture of Service

CHAPTER SEVEN

Start Good Rumors

*L*ooking for a doctor? Need a home loan? Buying a new car? Selecting a college? Where do you go for advice? Do you look in the paper? Watch TV? Or "Let your fingers do the walking"?

If you are like most people, you ask a family member, associate, or friend. Advertisers call this "word of mouth." It is the most effective way of advertising any organization—even a church! Word-of-mouth advertising is referred to in Scripture as a story, a report, a tiding, a reputation, and a rumor. Rumors are characterized as either good-speaking or evil-speaking (2 Cor. 6:8). Believers are encouraged to think about and spread good rumors (Phil. 4:8).

Jesus' ministry was predominantly communicated by word of mouth. After raising a dead man, Luke records that "this report [rumor, story] concerning Him went out all over Judea, and in all the surrounding district" (Luke 7:17). Jesus' reputation spread by positive word of mouth, and your church's ministry will too. Every day people talk about your church, its ministries, and programs. This talk adds to or subtracts from your reputation.

A classic example of how word-of-mouth advertising affects a church is found in 1 Thessalonians 1:8. Writing about the church in Thessalonica, Paul said, "For the word of the Lord has sounded forth [echoed] from you, not only in Macedonia and Achaia, but also in every place your faith toward God has gone forth." People were saying the Thessalonians had turned from idols to serve the living and true God. They were spreading the story by word of mouth. It was so effective that Paul confessed "we have no need to say anything."

My wife and I were spending a week at a church where I was candidating for the position of pastor. A real estate salesperson arranged for us to see several houses in the neighborhood where the church was located. My wife and the real estate agent were going through one house; and I decided to walk down the block, knock on a few doors, and simply ask people what they knew about the church. I introduced myself as someone who was thinking of purchasing a home and asked how they liked the area. After a little bit of conversation, I casually asked if they knew anything about the church a few blocks away. Some knew more than others, but everyone had heard something about the church. One lady said she had heard that the church was going to build a new facility on the vacant land next to it. Others offered insights such as, "It's rumored to be a nice family church," and, "They reportedly keep to themselves." A large number of the rumors I discovered that day were positive ones. I later accepted a call to pastor this church in part due to the reputation it had which I found that day talking to people in the neighborhood.

How Rumors Spread

Studies in the field of "Diffusion of Innovation" (how new products spread) have found that people do not choose a product purely on factual information. The overwhelming majority of people depend on subjective evaluations conveyed to them from other individuals like themselves who have previously adopted a product. It appears that potential "adopters" rely on the modeling of others who have already adopted a product. New products take off after interpersonal networks are activated to spread subjective, positive evaluations.

Churches grow as previous adopters (members and attenders) model their happiness by spreading good rumors (positive word-of-mouth evaluations) to those who are potential adopters (friends, family, and associates). The word of mouth develops an "echo effect" as it reverberates back and forth, spreading to others who may be interested in your church. Keep the following insights in mind as you consider the impact that circulating rumors have on your church and its ministry.

Little Things

Word of mouth is not based on one thing you do or don't do. It's the result of tens or hundreds of little things you do consistently well. Occasionally, short-term rumors may focus on one particular aspect of your ministry. The long-term rumors, or word-of-mouth conversation, changes slowly since it depends on the history of ministry found in your church over many years.

Managing Word of Mouth

You do not have to sit by and wait to hear what people say about you; you can take control by using some of the ideas in this chapter. Word of mouth can be managed. You cannot stop people from talking, thus you must begin to use proactive strategies to manage what people are saying.

Word-of-Mouth Enhancement

Word of mouth does not replace anything you are doing. It supplements and enhances your current efforts in all areas of ministry. Talk alone will never be enough. Ralph Waldo Emerson reportedly told an acquaintance, "What you are speaks so loud, I can't hear what you say."

The 3-33 Rule

The rule of 3-33 is always at work. For every three people willing to tell a positive story about an experience with your church, there are thirty-three others who will tell a horror story.[1] For some reason, negative talk reaches a wider audience than positive talk. Since human nature tends to change little from one organization to another, it is likely that the figures presented by secular organizations are representative to those found in churches also.

> The White House Office of Consumer Affairs finds that a dissatisfied customer reveals the unpleasant experience to nine others. A California market research firm shows that dissatisfied automobile customers tell their stories to 22 others. A Dallas researcher says that in banking, a dissatisfied depositor will tell 11 others about a bank mistake and that those 11 tell five more people—average of 55 horror stories.[2]

People seem conditioned to share the negative aspects of their experiences. It takes about one hundred positive forces to overcome one negative force. How many positive stories about your church does it take to overcome the results of just one negative story carried along by word of mouth in your community?

The Talk Factor

Formal Talk—Public talk generated by a church about itself.

♦   Pastor Talk: When the pastor talks, everyone listens. He sets the tone for all other talk in the church. It is his job to talk about the purpose, mission, and values of the church. Pastor talk lets people know where the church is and where it is going. His talk must be carefully spoken since people are always trying to read between the lines to decipher what the pastor really means.

♦ Staff Talk: Staff talk should always be supportive of each other and the overall direction of the church. It is the job of each staff person to communicate the direction of their ministry focus, specifically relating how it assists in fulfilling the larger purpose, mission, and values of the church.

♦ Leader Talk: Comments made in board and committee meetings are the most powerful formal talk generated by church leaders. People look for clues from leaders that everything is going well.

Informal Talk—Nonpublic talk expresses the impressions people have of the church's formal talk.

♦ Grapevine Talk: Private talk between people about your church. A continuous defining and redefining of information both within and without your church. It may be positive or negative.

♦ Rumor Talk: Talk focusing on a particular issue that moves across the grapevine. Rumor talk tends to be emotional and often negative—but not always.

♦ Gossip Talk: Talk focusing on private matters, often with a negative flavor to it.

♦ Family Talk: Talk that takes place among spouses and children about your church.

Tools of Talk

♦ Ministry Talk: Unspoken impressions generated from programs and ministries which the church offers.

- Visual Talk: Unspoken impressions generated from the visual impact of the building, landscaping, and interior design.

- Memo Talk: Small formal notes circulated for the purpose of sharing information.

- Newsletter Talk: Regular newsletter distributed to keep people abreast of social and church information.

- Announcement Talk: Information shared in public concerning events and activities of the church.

- Advertising Talk: Brochures, direct-mail pieces, Yellow Pages ads, and ads in newspapers telling people outside your church about your ministry.

- Training Talk: Training events you offer to your people to teach ministry skills or procedures.

- Meeting Talk: Oral distribution of information done in a formal setting.

- Financial Talk: Budgets, balance sheets, year-end reports, and other information having to do with finances and an interpretation of your financial state.

- Signage Talk: Signs, logos, and symbols that communicate an official visual impression about your church.

- Letter Talk: Your church's official letterhead, logo, fax cover sheet, labels, and business correspondence.

- Phone Talk: The way people answer your phone and treat callers.

- Answering Machine Talk: The message given on your answering machine and the response it creates.

It's a Small World

Word-of-mouth talk travels fast. Sociologists think that the average person's sphere of influence includes 250 people.

This means that if your city has a population of 62,500, you are only two people away from everyone in town by word of mouth. If you tell all 250 people in your sphere of influence and they in turn tell all 250 people in theirs, then everyone in town will know what you talked about (250 X 250 = 62,500). Extending this formula two more steps reveals that each of us is only about four or five people removed from everyone in the entire world, which is the reason we often say, "It's a small world." It honestly is small by word of mouth.

The Second Mile

Positive word of mouth takes place when you exceed what people expect. Think of the service you offer to people as a continuum (see figure below). Not surprisingly, poor service results in negative word of mouth. What may shock you is to learn that just doing what people expect results in no word of mouth.

If you only do what people expect you to do, they won't talk about it since they expect that level of service. It's nothing special. It's when people receive more service than they expect that they spread good rumors. Excellent service results in positive word of mouth as people express to others their unexpected pleasure of being served well by your church.

Natural Word-of-Mouth Exposure

Some churches have natural word-of-mouth exposure due to their size. In general, a church with a worship attendance above that of the average church in its ministry area will have strong visibility by word of mouth. Note the following graph as an example.

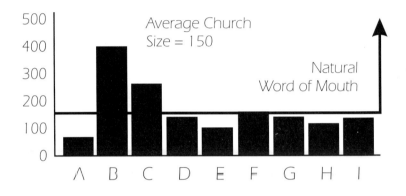

There are ten churches depicted above. The average worship attendance used in the example is 150. In order for a church to have natural word-of-mouth exposure, it will need to have a worship attendance above 150. It is easy to see that churches "B," and "C" are above this 150 line and will have a natural visibility via word-of-mouth. Church "F" is just at the breaking point of discovering that word of mouth happens quite naturally. The remaining churches will need to work at developing word-of-mouth advertising since they have too few people for such visibility to develop naturally.

If your church's worship attendance is below the average attendance of all the other churches in your ministry area, then developing positive word-of-mouth talk will be an important factor in the future growth of your church. You also need to give serious consideration to this aspect of your ministry if your present word of mouth is negative or weak. Does your church have natural word-of-mouth visibility in its ministry area? If not, then you will need to develop a strategy to help increase your word-of-mouth image. Here are some ideas to energize good rumors about your church.

Energizing Good Rumors

How may a church tie into the network of current adopters (church members and attenders) to reach potential adopters? As a church leader, you do not need to passively sit by. You can be thoughtful, organized, and systematic about word-of-mouth advertising. Good rumors will develop as present members and attenders sense personal satisfaction with the ministry of your church. Begin by listening to what your members are saying. Energizing good rumors about your church begins inside your church. The word of mouth that is generated by your present members and regular worshipers is a powerful influence on the morale, ministry, and mission of your church. What do your members say about your church to other members? What are they communicating to those outside your church? If you don't know, find out.

Avoid Negative Talk

Negative talk about your church must be avoided no matter how difficult conditions are. When I was a soccer coach, my number one rule was "never say anything bad about your teammate." The minute teammates start speaking negatively about their team and each other is the moment the team begins to fall apart. By sacrificially serving each other, we work together to fulfill Christ's command to make disciples of all the nations.

Negative talk about each other and our church, even innocently, causes serious damage. Once our members start bad-mouthing our church, nonmembers pick it up and pass it along with more fury since they heard it right from the source. Make it clear to people what the Bible says about negative talk (see James 3:1–13) and how it affects the growth of your church. Train them to say the right things. Show them the proper way to bring disagreements to the church leadership. Don't bad-mouth other churches from your pulpit.

Preach the positive side of things more than the negative. You don't need to be blind to or totally ignore the negatives, but always create an atmosphere that stresses the positive, more productive side.

Share Good News about Your Church

A newsletter is a solid way to build a network of loyal followers. It is time consuming but is certainly worth the effort. One key is regularity. Many churches put out a newsletter sporadically. If anything, this works against the development of good rumors. Make good use of pictures. Keep it crisp, clean, clear, and upbeat. Feature stories that share good news about what is happening in your ministry. Be especially alert to stories about people who illustrate your culture of loving care and service to each other. Interviewing people from the platform on Sunday mornings is another way to share good stories about your church. Select new people, those with a fresh testimony and those who have been served effectively by your church. Host an end-of-the-year event where many people who have been touched by your church may share their stories. As members hear these real stories they will naturally share them by word of mouth to others, thus passing on the good news about your church's ministry.

Reach Out to Community Leaders

One pastor visited the mayor of his city. After the proper introductions were made, the mayor asked how he could help the pastor. The pastor confided that he simply wanted to know how the mayor was doing. Before leaving, he prayed for the mayor! The mayor was shocked and pleased. Needless to say, this opinion leader has good things to say about this pastor and his church. Host a thank-you dinner for other community leaders such as fire fighters, police officers, city council members—not as events to register complaints but to thank them for a job well done for the people of your city or community.

Build Good Experiences and Memories

The DWYPYWD principle builds trust and positive word of mouth. What does it mean? "Do what you promised you would do." Complete projects that are started. Work on small goals that are sure to succeed and publicize it when they are met. Take slides and pictures of church events. Show them at meetings throughout the year. Develop a video about your church. Host open houses where members may share their desires, hopes, and concerns. At the same meetings church leaders may communicate the church's vision and direction, thereby starting good rumors that will be shared again and again. Remove negative signs from your church property and literature. Look around your church and see how many times you count the word *no.* Do you have signs that say:

No Smoking

No Parking

No Skateboarding

No Dancing

No Running

No Food or Beverages Allowed?

If you have these and others hanging on your walls or posted on your property, take them down. If they are printed in your bulletin, program, or newsletter, take them out. It is difficult to build positive word of mouth about your church if roadblocks such as these shout a negative message.

Communicate Victories

Print answers to prayer. Share how your church is progressing toward its yearly goals. Tell how ministries are reaching people. Publicly read thank-you cards and letters from people who have been helped by your church. Develop a sense of expectancy by preaching messages that point to hope in the Lord. Describe how God has met church needs over the years and project His certain help in the future. Tell how God has answered your prayers.

Provide Business Cards

Give each person, including children, in your church fifty-two cards. *Everyone* is important enough for this tiny investment. Encourage people to hand out one card each week with an invitation to attend your worship services. People feel important when they have a card, and they'll use it to spread the good word about your church. Not only will they hand them to family and friends, but the cards will start showing up in other places too. People will give them to their mail carrier, gas station attendant, and dentist. The first time you find a guest who came as a result of the business card be sure to make it well known.

Exceed Expectations

Wal-Mart has hired older people to stand at the doors to greet people as they come in. These grandfatherly and grand-motherly people make a special fuss over children and offer you a friendly greeting along with a shopping cart. This service went beyond what anyone expected at the time. Now other stores are offering the same service. Why not hand out a rose to each lady who attends your church, not just on Mother's Day, but other Sundays too. Prepare a special coloring book for children. Don't just buy one; have one designed with a story about your church and your children's ministry. Then, give each child a small box of crayons and your coloring book as a special gift. Take a video of the children doing something special during Sunday School, then show it after church on several televisions near your refreshment table. Give copies to all parents who want one.

For certain, we know that people tell others—lots of others—about their experience at your church. The only action you can take to create positive word of mouth is to offer a ministry that makes every person extraordinarily happy. This happens only when a church has a culture of service.

Spreading the Word—A Summary

♦ Word-of-mouth advertising is the most effective way to communicate your church's commitment to service. The earthly ministry of Jesus and the church of Thessalonica illustrate instances of word of mouth being used in the Bible.

♦ Studies have found that knowledge of products and organizations spread rapidly when an "echo effect" occurs. An echo effect takes place when word of mouth reverberates back and forth between people talking about a product, organizations—even a church.

♦ Seven principles help understand word of mouth:

1. Short-term word of mouth may focus on a particular aspect of a church's ministry. It is long-term word of mouth built over years of positive ministry that is most effective, however.

2. Word of mouth can be managed.

3. Word of mouth does not replace anything you are already doing, it just supplements your ministry.

4. The rule of 3-33 is always at work. For every three people who are willing to tell a positive story about your church, another thirty-three are willing to tell a negative one.

5. Word of mouth spreads quickly since people have an average of 250 people in their sphere of influence.

6. Positive word of mouth occurs when your church serves people by doing more than they expect you to do.

7. Churches with an average worship attendance above the average of all churches in their ministry area have natural word-of-mouth advertising due to their size. Smaller churches must work extra hard to make themselves known.

♦ Positive word-of-mouth rumors can be energized in your church by:
  — teaching people to avoid negative talk;
  — sharing good news about your church as it happens;
  — ministering to community leaders;
  — building good experiences and memories for your people;
  — communicating victories and answers to prayer;
  — providing business cards to every person;
  — exceeding expectations by doing something special.

Something to Think About

For every three people willing to tell a positive story about your church,
thirty-three are willing to tell a negative one.

Look for Signs of No

Spend some time looking over your church's literature and signs posted on walls and church grounds. Do you have signs with the word no in them such as:

No Smoking
No Skateboarding
No Parking
No Dancing
No Food or Beverages
No Running
No Talking?

Are there other ways you may be saying no to people? What variations of these and other signs are found around your church? What is the message they are saying to people? Are there ways to say the same message in a positive manner?

One Little Thing

Launch a "One Little Thing" program for your church. Print a card like the following.

Then collect the cards and begin doing the little things.

One Little Thing

It often takes just one little thing to make a church more effective. Please complete the following two statements and return as instructed.

One thing I hear others say about our church is: _____

_____

_____

One little thing we could do to address this comment is:

_____

_____

CHAPTER EIGHT

Say Hello
to Your Community

Good doctrine, good fellowship, good prayer, and good ministry—do they guarantee the growth of a church? Not necessarily.

Sometimes churches do not do well, even though they have the basic ingredients. One problem is that they often are not communicating well to their target audience. Potential guests do not clearly understand "who" and "what" they are. They lack image.

Image is an intangible but important part of a church's growth strategy. All the visual symbols of a church—logos, signs, letterheads, advertisements, and facilities—come together to form one unified picture. How is an image created? One way is through advertising. *Webster's New World Dictionary* offers as one definition for *image:* "impression by the general public, often one deliberately created or modified by publicity, advertising."

Not long ago pastors and church leaders refused to use mass media. The typical attitude toward Madison Avenue made advertising techniques appear immoral or manipulative. Today, however, many churches and leaders are using direct mail, telemarketing, and newspaper advertising in an effort to communicate their ministry to those outside the church. Letting people know that your church is ready to serve them is vital to attracting new guests.

I doubt that any of the New Testament churches had a brochure or direct mail campaign. However, they did create an atmosphere where growth occurred. Often the means they used were what we would call advertising.

The personal letters of the New Testament are an obvious advertising medium—direct mail, in our terms. Luke, John, James, Peter, and Paul all used this advertising tool to communicate their love, care, teachings, and exhortation to people who could not be reached in any other way.

Word-of-mouth advertising was instrumental in reaching unchurched people around Thessalonica. "For the word of the Lord has sounded forth from you," Paul stated, "not only in Macedonia and Achaia, but also in every place your faith toward God has gone forth, so that we have no need to say anything" (1 Thess. 1:8).

Actually the Bible was the first printed piece of advertising. Consider the familiar John 3:16: "For God so loved the world, that He gave His only begotten Son, that whoever believes in Him should not perish, but have eternal life." All the elements of advertising are found in this verse. The Product: Jesus Christ. The Price: Free. The Promise: Eternal Life. *Guaranteed!* God was the very first advertiser. The principles of advertising were created by God Himself!

What Advertising Will and Won't Do

You say you don't advertise? Wrong! You advertise in hundreds of ways every day through your facilities, grounds, signs, and the transactions your members make with their neighbors, friends, and family members.

While not a remedy for all church ills, advertising can be a major part of a church growth mix. Advertising will build morale. A positive advertising strategy can raise members' morale and give them a point of reference for inviting others to church.

Advertising will create a climate for growth. Through advertising, potential guests can learn of the opportunity for a personal and rewarding relationship with the living God. They can learn of a church's desire to meet their needs. They can learn of a church's openness to new people.

Advertising will attract guests. Advertising can create an inviting image and communicate specific opportunities, times, dates, and places for involvement.

Advertising will shape community attitudes. Advertising offers a church the opportunity to tell the community what it wants them to know. Such ideals as a desire to be helpful, assurance of acceptance, the enthusiasm of present members, and the sense of fulfillment Christ brings to life may be communicated through mass media techniques.

While advertising is one method that can be used to communicate the good news, it is not a get-rich-quick gimmick.

Advertising will not change reality. Once the public visits, they will find out if the experience lives up to the story. False advertising may get people to attend a church service, but only one time.

Advertising will not convert people. Even though the gospel is a simple message, advertising is too simplistic to give a full understanding which will lead to personal commitment.

Advertising will not cause personal growth. Growth occurs over time as people learn, apply truth, and experience life. At the most, advertising can inform persons of an opportunity that will help them grow.

Advertising will not replace personal relationships. Satisfied customers who tell others about a product are the best advertising available. Andrew told Peter. Philip found Nathanael. Cornelius gathered his relatives and close friends. Word of mouth is always the key.

How to Begin

Every church begins at square one with the ability and the right to tell others about itself. Your church begins by telling others what you stand for, what you will deliver, and how you will do it. People generally believe what you say about yourself, at least until they come to see for themselves. Expectations lead to people's perceptions. Once you establish expectations, your reputation is on the line. People will expect you to live up to what you say about yourself.

Concerned leaders should begin by building a strong commitment to the Great Commission in your church. The energy and cost of developing a solid advertising strategy finds support among those who care deeply about telling their communities about Christ. Without this foundational belief, advertising will be a short-sighted investment bringing limited results.

Determine your ministry area and focus advertising within this limited geographical area for best results. A ministry area is the geographical area from which a church draws most of its worshipers. This can be determined by placing a pin on a map where your church is located. Then add more pins showing where your worshipers live. A visual picture will develop of your prime ministry area. Or you can call the local planning department of your city or county and ask them what the average trip time is in your community. Most churches will discover that average trip time falls between ten and twenty minutes. This means that people generally travel that amount of time to go shopping, drive to work, or attend church. Drawing a circle around your church on a map equal to about an average trip time away from your building will give you a fair idea of your ministry area.

Select your target audiences. Direct different strategies to current members, church shoppers, and the unchurched population you are trying to attract. Research the needs, attitudes, and concerns of your target groups.

Develop a communications team of an editor, writer, artist, and photographer. Balance your strategy inward to church members and outward to potential contacts. Regularly communicate through the use of a newsletter within the church. Cultivate positive word-of-mouth communication and fashion an advertising campaign for those outside the church. Invest 5 percent of your total budget per year in a total advertising plan. Don't give up after the first try. A well-developed image unfolds over several years.

Selecting a New Church Name

Saying hello to your community begins with a good church name. Many churches are named to signify a place, like Main Street Church. Others are named to designate a denominational affiliation, like Faith Baptist Church. Other names, such as Community Bible Church, open broad doors, while some names hold out spiritual ideals, like Church of the Open Door. Many church names present biblical pictures, like Good Shepherd Lutheran Church. Some contain nearly an entire system of theology, like Pillar of Fire Mount Zion Holiness Church of the Straight Gate. Whatever name a church has, a good name is better than a bad one; and a great name can open doors to its unreached community by communicating the desire of the church to be of service to others.

Today many churches are changing their names. To some, this is a new concept. Yet changing a church name is not as new as many people might think. For instance, the vast majority of early Americans were Anglicans. In fact, two-thirds of the signers of the Declaration of Independence were Anglicans, as were George Washington, John Madison, Patrick Henry, Alexander Hamilton, and John Marshall. After the American Revolution, the Anglicans lost their dominant position. Since the Anglican Church was identified with England, thousands of Americans left to become part of the free churches that reflected America's zeal for freedom. Not until the Anglicans renamed themselves the Protestant Episcopal Church were they able to enjoy growth again.

Why Change Your Name?

Why would anyone want to change a church's name? Here are four reasons some are choosing to do so.

A New Location. When Park Street Church moves to Fifth Avenue, it will need to change its name or suffer a loss of identity. If the name is not changed, there will be increased confusion as new people move into the community and are unaware that Park Street Church is now located on Fifth Avenue.

A New Target. The First German Baptist Church initially ministered to a primarily German audience. Over the years, however, the community has changed and a new target audience must be reached. Without a name change, it is unlikely that people of other ethnic descents will visit.

A New Identity. Twenty years ago Broadway Presbyterian Church struggled through difficult times. Many people left and joined other churches in the local area. Broadway is now experiencing love and peace within its membership. Yet its previous reputation lives on. A name change is one way Broadway may clear away the old memories and create a new identity.

A New Direction. Faith Community Church organized a VISION 2000 team to redefine its mission and has decided to set a new direction for the future. Noting that their community has many hurting people, they elected to communicate their new desire to help with a new name—New Hope Community Church.

Seven Guidelines

If you think a new church name might help you advertise a new culture of service to your community, here are seven guidelines to think about as you work through the choices.

Choose a name that attracts the unchurched. One key to serving the unchurched is to use a church name that is understandable and attractive to them. Consider what unchurched people think about names like "Faith," "Grace," and other names with religious sounding connotations. Narrow your choice down to five names and then survey people in movie lines, ballparks, shopping malls, and by phone to see what they think of your choices.

Choose a name that sets you apart. Churches tend to choose similar names. One church realized that its name was like nine others in the same area. Ask yourself what causes your name to stand out. What makes your church unique? How is your church different from other churches with similar names?

Choose a name that is simple to remember. A cumbersome name must be classified along with a poor location or a run-down facility—each can be overcome, but it often takes extraordinary effort to do so. Keep your name short. Don't try to say too much in your name. One word is best, but two or three words are OK.

Choose a name that helps people find your church. One pastor jokingly said, "It takes Daniel Boone to find our church." His church, like many, was established in a small, quiet neighborhood which today is off the beaten path. Help people locate your church by naming it after a street, a local attraction, a physical landmark or other unique feature.

Choose a name that removes barriers. Some people remember churches as places with long lists of "don'ts." People shouldn't trip over your theology because of what your name suggests. Look at a potential name through unchurched eyes. Ask unchurched people to give you their first response upon hearing your new name. Hire a consulting firm to investigate possible new names for you and make a recommendation on which one to select.

Choose a name that expands your potential. Don't limit your drawing power to one city or geographical area unless there is tremendous potential for growth in that area. Select a name broad enough to include an entire city rather than simply a neighborhood; a name with wide appeal rather than a limited appeal; a name that communicates to a larger audience rather than a smaller one.

Choose a name that communicates vibrancy. Church names that communicate excitement and celebration are attractive to people who are hurting and in need of support. Use a name that includes words like *hope* or *life.* Try using the word *new* since people like to be part of a pioneering venture. Ask if your name communicates excitement.

Check with your denominational leaders to see what, if any, regulations they have concerning your name. Take the proper legal steps to file a name change with your state government. Change all the items containing your old name, such as church stationery, bulletins, programs, business cards, brochures, and church signs. Don't wait until you use up all the old stationery. If a name change is important to make, it is important to change it throughout.

A First Impression Piece

The church was ready to close its doors. New guests seldom visited. Morale was too low to encourage significant word-of-mouth exposure of the church's ministry among the unchurched. We didn't have much money, but I determined we would do something to reach our community. The answer was a First Impression Piece. We designed an introductory brochure about our church and began mailing it to every home in our ministry area. At first we only had enough money to mail to about two hundred homes a month. So every month, without fail, we systematically mailed it to those in our area. We did this for five years, and it paid off in more guests visiting our church. It is a great way to say hello to your community.

A First Impression Piece is a brochure that is given to new people as a way to briefly inform them about your church. The cover of your First Impression Piece must be designed to catch the attention of as many readers as possible to draw them into the rest of the piece. Four out of five readers will only look at the first page. A cover should include a photo or drawing that illustrates your purpose or mission. Use pictures of people, *not* buildings. Select a title that implies a benefit. For example, "New Hope: The Friendly Church that Cares" implies that there is hope, friendship, and concern at that church. Or "Catch the Spirit of New Life at Community Presbyterian Church" implies an exciting new approach to life. Design an up-to-date church logo. Ask an artist or print professional to review your logo and to make suggestions on modernizing it. Consider the design, color, understandability, and so forth. Include a statement that notes some benefits of your church. Why would anyone want to come? What benefits will they receive by attending your church?

The main part of your First Impression Piece should give people an overview of your church. Resist the desire to say everything. This is just a "first" impression piece. If it does its job, you will have further opportunities to tell more of your story to the people who begin attending your church. The copy should be readable with loose, not "packed," text, written in the everyday language of the readers. Use pictures and titles that are understandable to the primary audience you are targeting. Mention the benefits and special features of your church. A short biography or sketch of your senior pastor and staff photos are always appropriate. As space permits, try using short testimonials from various people in your church, with their pictures if possible. A statement of your church's purpose or mission written in common language (twenty-five words or less), a simple map showing your church's location, and an overview of your church facilities (essential for larger churches with complex facilities) are good additions. Also consider including:

- a description of programs and activities for every age group;
- photos of your congregation participating in worship and other activities;
- first impression stories of how people in your church are being served;
- photos and descriptions of your church's service to the community at large;
- a brief schedule of activities;
- an invitation to visit;
- offers of professional help or service.

Design your First Impression Piece so that it may be used in a variety of ways. It should be sized to fit into a standard business envelope and should include a mailing panel so that it may be mailed individually. Be sure to include your church's name, complete address, and phone number. Include postal codes and area codes, as well as the times of your programs and location.

A well-designed First Impression Piece is the cornerstone of a church advertising plan. Once it has been designed, plan on mailing it to every home in your ministry area. Mail it out every year either in September or January. If funds are available, mail the First Impression Piece to everyone in your ministry area at once. Do this every year without fail, since it takes time to catch the attention of those in your community.

Some churches won't have enough money. If that's your case, you can do this gradually. The first year you will mail the First Impression Piece to everyone within a five-minute drive of your church building. The second year mail it to everyone within a ten-minute drive. Continue in the third year by sending it to everyone within a fifteen-minute drive. In the fourth year mail it to everyone within a twenty-minute drive. What do you do in the fifth year? Redesign your First Impression Piece and start all over again.

The biggest mistake churches make with direct mail is to try it once and forget it. What you ultimately hope to accomplish is the imprinting of your name and ministry in people's minds so that, when they do want to attend church, they think of your church. Saying hello to your community takes time and patience. Keep mailing First Impression Pieces into their homes. It will create results.

Other forms of advertising are also great ways to reach new people; *newspaper ads,* for example. In developing your ads, remember: (1) Focus on issues that unchurched people are concerned with. Do some personal interviews and research on your "target audience." (2) Write the ad in the language of the audience you intend to reach. Show the copy to unchurched friends before you run it to see if it communicates and elicits the desired response. (3) Don't place the ad on the church page. Place it in the paper where your "target group" is most likely to read it.

Phone Book Ad Re-do

Phone book display ads are expensive, and represent a long-term commitment. Unfortunately, many lack the impact that would make them effective. In the "before and after" example that follows on the next two pages, notice how much stronger the phone book ad becomes with a few simple changes.

The "flag" or church name is offered in an interesting font, but is ill placed

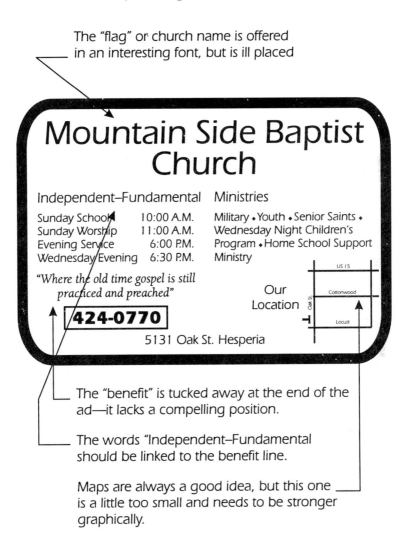

Mountain Side Baptist Church

Independent–Fundamental

Sunday School 10:00 A.M.
Sunday Worship 11:00 A.M.
Evening Service 6:00 P.M.
Wednesday Evening 6:30 P.M.

"Where the old time gospel is still practiced and preached"

424-0770

Ministries

Military • Youth • Senior Saints • Wednesday Night Children's Program • Home School Support Ministry

Our Location

US 15
Cottonwood
Oak St.
Locust

5131 Oak St. Hesperia

The "benefit" is tucked away at the end of the ad—it lacks a compelling position.

The words "Independent–Fundamental should be linked to the benefit line.

Maps are always a good idea, but this one is a little too small and needs to be stronger graphically.

The temptation to put the church's name at the top should be avoided. The church is the solution. The need should be listed first. Reverse type is employed to catch the eye of the reader.

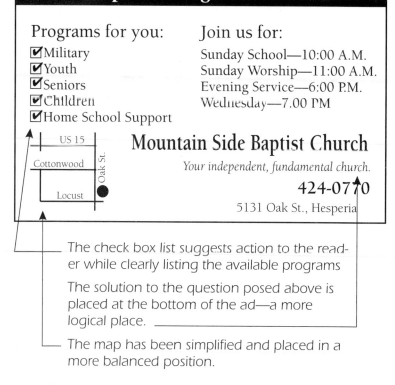

Looking for a church that offers the "old time" Gospel and "right now" life values?

Programs for you:

☑Military
☑Youth
☑Seniors
☑Children
☑Home School Support

Join us for:

Sunday School—10:00 A.M.
Sunday Worship—11:00 A.M.
Evening Service—6:00 P.M.
Wednesday—7.00 PM

US 15
Cottonwood
Oak St.
Locust

Mountain Side Baptist Church

Your independent, fundamental church.

424-0770

5131 Oak St., Hesperia

The check box list suggests action to the reader while clearly listing the available programs

The solution to the question posed above is placed at the bottom of the ad—a more logical place.

The map has been simplified and placed in a more balanced position.

Telemarketing is another possibility. In a mass-calling campaign expect to make ten thousand calls, have one thousand persons express interest, and see fifty to one hundred persons show up to your advertised event. A well-done *direct mail* piece will generate about a 2 percent response. One mistake churches make in using direct mail is not sending out enough pieces. A minimum mailing of 10,000 is needed to receive any measurable response. Mail at least three times a year: early fall, before Christmas, and before Easter.

Whichever form you use, aim to produce quality ads that are simple, creative, and memorable. If necessary, hire an advertising agency. See the costs as an investment. Advertising should have a "we-can-help" attitude (see the make over of a telephone book ad on page 128 as an example). Developing a church name that communicates your willingness to serve others and then saying hello through a First Impression Piece mailed to everyone in your ministry area are good ways to get started.

An Illustration

A story is told in advertising circles that a man found himself in an elevator with Lee Iacocca, then the head of the Chrysler Corporation.

"You're Lee Iacocca, aren't you?" asked the man.

The auto exec acknowledged that he was.

"Mr. Iacocca," the man spoke up, "I want to tell you how much I enjoy your television commercials."

To this compliment Iacocca replied, "Sir, I could care less what you think of my commercials. What I want to know is, what kind of car do you drive?"

If people don't buy the car, the commercials don't matter. A good church name and a nice First Impression Piece are all desirable for a church. Yet if people don't buy the product—life in Christ—it doesn't matter. Bear in mind that the important thing is not the advertising but the response.

Telling Our Story—A Summary

♦ Good doctrine, good fellowship, good prayer, and good ministry are important to church growth. If your church isn't communicating well to its audience, however, these ingredients may not be enough.

- What advertising will not do:
  It will not change reality.
  It will not convert people.
  It will not cause personal growth.
  It will not replace personal relationships.

- What advertising will do:
  It will build the morale of your people.
  It will create a climate for growth.
  It will attract guests one time.
  It will shape community attitudes about your church.

- Before you begin, focus on developing a commitment to the Great Commission, determine your ministry area, and carefully select specific target groups of people to reach.

- Saying hello to your community begins by choosing a good church name.
  Choose a name that attracts the unchurched.
  Choose a name that sets you apart.
  Choose a name that is simple to remember.
  Choose a name that helps people find your church.
  Choose a name that removes barriers to guests.
  Choose a name that expands your potential.
  Choose a name that communicates vibrancy.

- Design, print, and mail a First Impression Piece to every home in your ministry area on a systematic schedule. Use the piece for five years and then redesign it and begin mailing to all homes again.

———

Something to Think About

If you think you don't advertise, you're wrong!
Your church advertises in hundreds of ways every day
through its facilities, grounds, signs, and the transactions its

members make with neighbors, friends, and family members. The question is not "Do you advertise?" It's "What are you communicating to others?"

Before You Write a Word

Before you contact a graphic artist or write a word of copy for your brochure, answer the following questions:

1. What is the purpose of your church?_____

_____

_____

2. What makes your church unique in contrast to other churches in your ministry area?_____

_____

_____

3. What are some benefits that people could expect to receive from attending your church?_____

_____

_____

4. What are the newer members saying about your church?_____

_____

_____

5. What is the primary audience you hope to reach with this advertising piece? (Families, youth, elderly, singles, particular ethnic group, or others.)_____

_____

_____

6. What do you want the reader to know, think, feel, and do after reading your First Impression Piece?_____

_____

_____

7. What resources do you have available for producing this piece? (Budget, time, people who can help, equipment, final authority for approvals.)_____

_____

What's in a Name?

Conduct your own survey.

1. Make a list of the names of all churches in your ministry area. _____

_____

_____

_____

2. Group the list of names based on similarity. For example, all church names with "Grace" in them go in one category, all those with "Community" go in another, and so forth. Some names may appear in more than one category._____

_____

_____

_____

3. How many other churches have a name similar to yours? The more there are, the greater likelihood there is confusion about your church's identity in your ministry area. _____

_____

_____

_____

4. Look at your name from unchurched persons' perspective. What does your name say to them? What doesn't it say that you wish it did say?_____

_____

_____

5. Are there any barriers in your name that might keep people from visiting? (A good way to analyze this is to ask some unchurched people what they think about your name.)_____

_____

_____

Summarize your findings._____

_____

_____

_____

PART FOUR

Practicing a Culture of Service

CHAPTER NINE

Reach Out
and Touch Someone

We use them in our cars, airplanes, golf carts, and even in our backyards. We use them to say, "I love you," to shop for gifts, to summon the paramedics, and to get the latest scores of our favorite teams. Now we are using them for church ministry. What are they? Telephones!

On March 7, 1876, the telephone was considered the most valuable patent ever issued. It's hard to believe, but back in 1879 the first telephone operators had to memorize the names of subscribers! A measles epidemic changed all that when a doctor recommended assigning numbers to the townspeople in case the operator got ill. Today the telephone is so ingrained in our lives that it is almost unthinkable to do without one.

In 1955 many churches began using the telephone for ministry by continuously broadcasting recorded prayers over the telephone. By the early sixties, churches across the United States were offering "dial-a-prayer" service. New York's Fifth Avenue Presbyterian Church still uses this program and averages more than five hundred calls daily.

Churches now fax their Sunday School order to a company across the country. Church secretaries correspond to pastors via cellular phones. You can even order your staff luncheons by fax from the local deli. And what about that portable, wireless phone that is the size of last year's pocket calculator? You don't have one yet?

The Telephone as a Tool

The telephone is a super example of how churches are developing new ways of effectively serving people—Christians and non-Christians. Telemarketing has become a predominant means of planting new churches and reaching out to the unchurched.

With home visitation declining because of increased neighborhood crime, commuting, and the saturation of contacts experienced in everyday life, there is a resistance to anyone stopping by for an unannounced visit. In response many churches are using the telephone as a means of pastoral care for their members.

It has been discovered that phone calls have about the same appeal as a personal visit. A phone call offers the contact, the encouragement, and the image of a visit, while respecting people's personal time. Churches are using personal phone calls to follow up guests and perform basic pastoral care. It is another form of care that transcends pastoral and lay visitation.

"Telecare" is the name given to pastoral care completed by phone. You might consider using this means of providing basic care for your people. Here are a few steps to implementation. Identify callers and select key leadership to oversee the program. Choose those who like to talk on the phone. Recruit people by phone to hear how they sound. Don't overlook shut-ins as possible callers.

Train callers in short sessions of about two hours. Teach people to understand the power of words, listening skills, and how to keep a record of their call. Practice by having callers phone each other in different offices at church. Provide a basic outline of questions to ask or ideas to talk about.

Find some phones. Use the phones at the home of the caller. Allow callers to do their work at the church using church phones. Install an extra line at church that is dedicated for pastoral care.

Contact active and inactive members, shut-ins and teenagers, excited people and apathetic people, quiet ones and compulsive talkers. As people continue to withdraw, the church is going to play a vital role in overcoming the loneliness that will result. The telephone may be an instrument your church can use to reach out and touch someone.

Starting New Ministries

The coming decade will see continued development of ministry by telephone. Telecare is just one example of a new form of ministry being used to serve others with the love of Christ. There are countless ways to serve people. Long ago Christ called His disciples' attention to the readiness of others to learn about the gospel. Casting His eyes toward a group walking on a road, He directed attention to them with these words: "The harvest is plentiful, but the workers are few. Therefore beseech the Lord of the harvest to send out workers into His harvest" (Matt. 9:37–38).

Seven Questions

The harvest is ready. People are open and eager to respond. We just need to open our eyes and begin looking for them. Thus, a goal of our culture of service must be to reach out and touch new people. In most cases it requires starting new ministries to attract new people and give them an opportunity for the love of Christ to be shown. But what ministry should you start? Ask these seven questions.

1. *"Where do we sense the burden of God in our church at this time?"* The number one attitude seen in a church with a culture of service is the desire to reach out to others. Caring service is the center of all that they do. Not surprisingly, the beginning of a ministry which will serve others is a growing burden from God.

A church desiring to serve others should seek God's leading and wisdom and carefully evaluate resources and abilities to implement a new ministry. God desires to use our gifts and abilities to serve others. Carl George, director of the Charles E. Fuller Institute for Evangelism and Church Growth, notes that in Luke 10:25–37, Jesus tells us not to ask, "Whom am I required to love?" ("Who is my neighbor?"), but "How may I show the love of Christ to others?" ("To whom am I a neighbor?").

2. *"What specific group of people is God giving us a burden to serve?"* Different people have different needs. Gone are the days of thinking broadly. It is now time to think specifically. At one time churches developed a one-size-fits-all ministry for adults. Later we added a ministry for younger adults, middle-aged adults, and senior adults. Now we must view adult ministry even more specifically.

Young adults can be divided into several categories such as collegians, career singles, young couples without children, young couples with children, and single parents. Middle-aged adults can be never-married singles, couples with elementary school children, couples with junior-highers, couples with senior-highers, couples with college-age children, empty-nest couples, and single parents. Older adults include the recently retired, adults living in care facilities, adults living with their children, adults raising their grandchildren, and on and on. A church cannot say it wants to minister to adults. Today you must be very specific naming a special type of adult.

3. *"What needs do these people have that we could meet?"* If you don't know what their needs are, ask them. Sticking to your own idea of what people want without asking them for their input is a mistake.

Years ago my church tried to begin a coffeehouse for local college students as a means of serving them and sharing the good news of Jesus Christ. It was called "The Out House Coffeehouse." We just assumed they wanted a coffeehouse and moved quickly forward with our plans never thinking to survey the college students in order to discover what their needs were.

As you might guess, the coffeehouse ministry was a disaster. Even though the publicity, invitations, food, music, and people were all in place, no one came. It wasn't what the collegians needed or wanted. If we had asked them earlier, it would have saved us a great deal of time, effort, and money, not to mention the embarrassment we suffered.

New Ministry Policies of Perimeter Church

The following policies are intended to encourage the development of healthy and varied ministries. Please keep them in mind in all phases of your ministry.

1. Ministries are to be self-funded. Perimeter Church desires to start as many ministries as God leads its members. However, ministries can be stifled if they are dependant upon the appropriation of limited funds.

2. Ministries are to be self-led. The Holy Spirit will raise up leaders of ministries as He sees fit. For those desiring to start a ministry, the staff and officers are able to offer advice on possible leaders but cannot be held responsible to recruit.

3. Ministries are to be self-propagated. When it comes time for a leader to step aside, he or she and the team must find a replacement, with the advice of the staff and officers. If no one desires to take over, this may mean that the ministry has run its course for the present.

4. Ministry teams must avoid more trouble. As ministries of Perimeter Church reflect back upon the whole body, and ultimately upon Christ Himself, it is imperative that ministry teams should stay within the accepted doctrines of Perimeter Church.

5. Ministry leaders must be members of Perimeter Church. All who attend Perimeter are encouraged to be involved in ministry, whether or not they are members. However, to maintain proper standards of ministry, leaders must be held accountable to the officers of the church and therefore must be members.

—Perimeter Church, Atlanta, Georgia; quoted in *Healthy Cells: Nurture Groups and Ministry Teams* (1990), 15.

4. *"What specific ministry are we qualified to start that fits with God's burden and the people we wish to serve?"* We in the church like to think that we can care for everyone. In a general way we do care for people from the cradle to the grave. But when it comes to beginning a new ministry, we must think strategically.

The fields truly are ripe for harvest. People are hurting and need to be loved and served in a way that will draw them to the Great Shepherd—Jesus Christ. No church has all the necessary resources—money, people, time, knowledge, skill—to do everything that can be proposed. Thus, we need to investigate as many ministry opportunities as reasonable. Talk with the leaders doing the ministry and, if possible, even participate in the ministry for a short time. While you are doing your research, prayerfully ask God what He wants your church to do. The following list is offered by Carl George as some potential ministry areas you could consider. Look them over and ask God to burden you with the ones that your church should pursue.

Ministry Areas to Consider

__ Prison Ministry

__ Homeless

__ Abused Children

__ Unemployed

__ Abused Spouses

__ English as Second Language

__ Substance Abuse:
alcohol, eating disorders,
drugs, tobacco

__ International Students

__ Terminally Ill

__ Homosexuals

__ Single Parents

__ Unwed Mothers

__ Crisis Pregnancy

__ Financial Counseling

__ Prenatal/Postnatal

__ Medical Personnel

__ Mothers of Preschoolers

__ Elderly

__ Abortion

__ AIDS

__ Trauma Victims

__ Illiterate

__ Other "people groups":

   __ Athletes

   __ Executives

   __ International Executives

   __ Politicians

   __ Artists

   __ Homemakers

   __ Broadcast and Print Media

   __ Students

   __ University Faculty

__ Refugees

__ Premarital Counseling

__ Separated and Divorced

__ Handicapped

__ Hospital Visitation

__ Widows/Widowers

__ Orphans

__ Incest Victims

__ Hungry

__ Crisis Counseling

5. *"What similar ministries are already being done by other churches or individuals?"* A young seminary student and his wife approached me for advice in planting a new church.

During our conversation I learned that she was going to oversee the children's ministry. I suggested several churches with well-run children's ministries for her to visit. After seeing how others were doing this ministry, her entire outlook was changed and her vision was stretched of what she wanted to organize in the new church.

I still remember her telling me about a church that used a Sesame Street approach to children's ministry. The church had invested a great deal of money in remodeling a large educational room into a soundstage where actors, similar to those on Sesame Street, acted out Bible lessons teaching children in a format that held their attention. By visiting this church, the young wife had an entirely new idea of how to do a children's ministry. Once God gives you an idea of a ministry you could start, investigate other churches doing similar ministries. Talk with those involved. Learn what is working and not working. What types of responses, roadblocks, and problems might you expect? Learn all you can from these ministries.

6. *"What will be our strategy and plan?"* Study your target group and put together a plan to reach them beginning with a specific need. Everything doesn't need to be planned in order to start serving others, but do consider the resources of your people—time, commitment, knowledge, skills, and money. Do not allow your desire to know everything beforehand squelch the burden and momentum for ministry which has been growing. Learn by doing.

7. *"What process do we need to follow to get approval from our church?"* Understand and follow the process for approval from your church. Go ahead and start your ministry so that leaders will know you are serious and know what you are doing. Leaders need your suggestions, advice, and ideas. Some may even wish to get involved themselves. After approval, be certain to keep leaders informed on the ministry.

The AAAA Plan

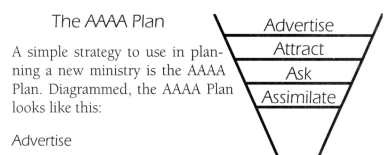

A simple strategy to use in planning a new ministry is the AAAA Plan. Diagrammed, the AAAA Plan looks like this:

Advertise

Begin by advertising your new ministry where the people you are trying to serve will be found. As an example, let's assume your church wants to reach young single mothers. After discovering that they are concerned with keeping their children off drugs, you might plan to offer a course on "How to Drug-Proof Your Child."

To attract them, you must advertise where single mothers will be found. Announcements on your church bulletin board or a flier in your church program probably won't find the audience you hope to reach. Instead, try placing your advertising in laundromats and day care centers. Distribute fliers at park playgrounds, in apartment complexes, and in grocery stores.

"Underpromise" in your advertising, and "overdeliver" in your ministry. There is nothing more important to the people you are trying to reach than seeing the promises you make are kept. People want churches to do what they say they are going to do. Keeping your word is worth more than all the smiles and donuts in the world. Advertising will bring people to you one time, but you must have the goods (the product) when they arrive, or they won't be back.

Attract

Attracting the people you want to serve initially happens by offering an event that speaks to a felt need in their lives. Young single mothers in large cities often fear the prospect of their children obtaining and using drugs, sometimes even in elementary school.

While their ultimate need is for salvation in Christ, they may not be attracted to a church offering them a Bible study in Genesis, even with free child care. Designing a course or event that speaks directly to a felt need in their lives has greater pulling power.

Attraction events should have an atmosphere that is non-churchy, nonformal, and nonthreatening. Prayers and religious sounding language, if used at all, should be used sparingly. Casual dress appropriate to the people you are serving and a location that is on their turf are best. New people are attracted to events that don't take up their entire day and that don't ask for long-term commitments. Short seminars or workshop presentations are most attractive.

Ask

To faithfully serve new people means moving past advertisement and attraction by asking participants to become involved in your new ministry. A three-hour seminar on "How to Drug-Proof Your Child" is only the start. Where the new ministry takes shape is by involving new people in longer-term relationships.

While some good tips can be learned in a short three-hour seminar, other needs and situations require long-term attention. By asking (inviting) those who participate in your attraction event to become involved in a small support group or other ministry, you begin the process of building a relationship that will lead many to Christ.

Assimilate

Assimilating the new people into the life of your church takes place naturally when people do three key things: develop friends in your church, join a group or class, and become involved in serving others.

By asking people to become involved in the support group, you complete two of these three things. People develop friends and have a group that they identify with. As you encourage them to find their own place of service in your group, they will be assimilated into the life of your church.[1]

Beginning New Ministries—A Summary

♦ Telecare is an example of a new form of ministry developed to reach people in our changing environment.

♦ In most cases, attracting new people requires the development of new ministries. The harvest is ready, but we need to open our eyes and see the opportunities to start new ministries.

♦ Ask the following seven questions to determine what new ministries to begin.

1. "Where do we sense the burden of God in our lives at this time?"

2. "What specific group of people is God giving us a burden to serve?"

3. "What needs do these people have that we could meet?"

4. "What specific ministry are we qualified to start that fits with God's burden and the needs of the people we wish to serve?"

5. "What similar ministries are already being done by other churches or individuals?"

6. "What will be our strategy and plan?"

7. "What process do we need to follow to obtain approval from our church?"

♦ Use the AAAA plan to get started.

—Advertise your new ministry where your target audience lives, works, and plays.

—Attract people to your new ministry by focusing on their felt needs. Design an event, class, or group that will begin to answer some of their questions, giving help and support in their area of need.

—Ask those who participate in your attraction event to become further involved in an ongoing ministry that will give additional answers and support to them.

—Assimilate new people into the life of your church by helping them make friends, stay involved in a group or class, and become involved in serving others themselves.

Something to Think About

*In most cases it will take new ministries
to reach new people for Christ.*

Looking at the Harvest

God has placed your church in a particular location among groups of people who are ripe for the harvest. Open your eyes and begin seeing the harvest around you by doing the following:

1. Take your church leaders on a tour of your community. Drive slowly through the community and make a list of the various people and potential needs you see.

2. Spend a week reading your local newspaper, jotting down the different groups of people and specific needs that are mentioned.

3. Make an appointment with your local fire chief, police chief, and mayor. When you meet with them, tell them your church is ready and willing to serve others in your community. Ask for ideas on how you can serve others.

4. Randomly call two hundred homes in your community, introduce yourself, and tell people your church wants to serve its community. Ask for ideas on needs and ways your church could be helpful to others.

5. Survey your own church members asking them to note the concerns and needs of people they know. Summarize your findings. What groups of people did you find? What are their needs? Which needs could your church begin to serve? Where has God directed your hearts?

Just Do It

1. What target group are you going to serve?_____

_____

_____

2. How do you plan to reach them?_____

_____

_____

3. What preparation have you done?_____

_____

_____

4. What resources do you need?_____

_____

_____

5. Who will serve with you?_____

_____

_____

6. When do you plan to start?_____

_____

_____

CHAPTER TEN

Welcome Guests Graciously

When I conduct a church growth consultation with a local church, I like to visit the church unannounced on a Sunday morning. This gives me the opportunity to feel the atmosphere of the worship service, observe the way newcomers are greeted, walk through the buildings, monitor traffic flow, and see the church through guest eyes.

In 1989 I visited a church with a worship attendance of 930. The large prominent buildings caught my attention as I drove into the parking lot. After finding a parking space close to a church entrance, I walked through the parking lot encountering many other people exiting their cars and heading into church. Since I had never been to this church before, I didn't know exactly where to enter the building, so I followed the general flow of traffic. Making my way into the patio area, I wandered through and around groups of people busily conversing with each other. Eventually I walked outside and around the perimeter of the church property. Along the way I encountered people coming and going to classes, the parking lot, and the sanctuary. Never once did anyone stop to talk to me. Some smiled as our eyes met, but not a single word was spoken. As I approached the back entrance I spotted the pastor standing outside with a cup of coffee in his hand greeting people excitedly. Drawing closer together he reached out his hand and whispered, "I hope I'm not the first one to greet you today." He was!

Guesterize Your Church

Being nice to people is just the beginning of building a great culture of service. The people I encountered were all nice people. They smiled at me. I had no reason to assume they were unkind. Yet, at the most, being nice and smiling accounts for only about 20 percent of a true culture of service. The important thing is to design systems that provide excellent service to those who attend our church. Nowhere is this more important than when we welcome newcomers on their first visit to our church. Systematic approaches to serving others is 80 percent of the battle. We must guesterize our church.

> Guest-er-ize (gest-er-ize), *vt.* to make a church more responsive to its guests and better able to attract new ones. *syn* see service, care, love, acceptance.

Guesterizing your church occurs when you make guests the most important people at your church on Sunday morning. It means responding to their needs in a manner that causes them to enjoy their experience. It means giving superior service so that they want to return the next week. To guesterize your church, I recommend the following principles.

Give Guests the Best Attitude

Guests to your church will immediately notice the prevailing attitude. Attitude is the tone one senses walking up to the church building, meeting others upon entering the front doors, sitting in the sanctuary, and talking with others. As mentioned in a previous chapter, most guests will make a judgment about your church within thirty seconds of entering the front door. Their judgment is not made on any scientific evidence slowly gathered over weeks, months, or even years. Their judgment is made quickly based on the attitude or atmosphere they experience. It is made subliminally within the first few moments that they experience our church.

One of the biggest needs people have is to know there is hope for tomorrow. They come to your church looking for encouragement. They want practical advice on how to make it through the week. They want to know that God has not given up on them.

The Bible, of course, is a book of hope. Its primary message is that God loves us and has a plan for our lives. It tells us that no matter how desperate our lives, God is in the picture making it turn out right (see Rom. 8:28). Do your preaching, music, friendliness, and people reflect an attitude of hope?

Atmosphere is also created by the facility. Stained-glass windows and dark wooden doors do not make for an initial open, friendly atmosphere. Clear glass doors and windows allow those walking up to or driving by the building to see inside, allowing for a more friendly feel. Small lobbies (foyers) feel cramped, often making a new person feel too exposed and under pressure. If you want to guesterize your church, I suggest you work on developing an atmosphere of hope and care in your church, as well as opening up your facility to make it feel warm and friendly.

Give Guests the Best Communication

As a church consultant, I visit several churches every year. One of my favorite techniques is to station myself in a busy part of the auditorium or foyer to see how many people will speak to me. In many cases, people will walk toward me, our eyes will meet, and then they will look toward the ground and walk on by. At other times they will smile as they go by. This makes your guests feel like nonpersons. They will not perceive you as a friendly church. If you want to guesterize your church, I suggest that you follow the "Ten-Foot Rule" and the "Just-Say-Hi Policy." Teach your people that whenever they come within ten feet of a person they don't know to just say, "Hi!" While this won't be an end to guesterizing your church, at least it will let newcomers know they are noticed.

Give Guests the Best Welcome

I was very tired. As I sat down in the auditorium my only desire was to be left alone to worship. To my horror the pastor asked all visitors to stand. Then one-by-one he went around the room asking each of us to introduce ourselves and to give a short word of greeting to the congregation. Even though I'm a seasoned churchgoer, it was more than embarrassing. I wondered how others felt. In today's society it's good to welcome guests from the pulpit but not to have them stand to be recognized. Give guests freedom to relax and enjoy the worship service. Whatever you do, take great pains not to embarrass the newcomer. Among other things this means you should not identify new people by placing a ribbon, flower, or name tag on them. Do not ask visitors to stand and speak before the entire congregation. A survey of one thousand adults eighteen years of age or older reported in 1994 that "making a speech" was the number one event causing adults to be nervous. It ranked first ahead of, in order: getting married, interviewing for a job, going to the dentist, a first date, and getting a divorce.[1] If you want to guesterize your church, I suggest you welcome guests but don't embarrass them in any way.

Give Guests the Best Parking

In our automobile age, three things continue to be true about most people. First, people don't like to walk more than one block to church. Second, people will drive around for several minutes to find a parking place closer to the entrance. Third, people who don't find a convenient parking space will drive on by without stopping.

If you want to guesterize your church, I suggest you reserve approximately 5 percent of your parking places for guests as close to your main entrance as possible. Clearly mark them for first- or second-time guests.

Give Guests the Best Seats

The most popular seats on an airplane are the aisle seats. The reason? People like to have a sense of openness rather than one of being trapped. We need intimate space—the immediate space around our bodies. Most of the time we guard this space allowing only privileged others to enter it. This is why we feel comfortable hugging a family member more than an individual we don't know well. New people who worship at our churches like to protect their intimate space. When we force them to sit close to another person or in the middle seats, it invades their intimate space and makes them uncomfortable. Unfortunately, they attribute their uncomfortableness to our church and are not likely to return.

The Ten Most Important People

In his excellent training manual for ushers and greeters, John Maxwell identifies the ten most important people Sunday morning in your church.

1. The Visitor. A visitor is the most important person that attends church on Sunday. His or her attendance has been motivated by a friend or a deep need. He brings his hurts, questions, and apprehensions. He looks for warmth, acceptance, and smiles. When he receives these things, he will return. When he returns, he will find God.

2. The Usher. The ushers are important because they are often the ones who have the first contact with people. They help people with directions. They are the ones who represent the church to newcomers. They maintain order in the church service, enabling it to flow smoothly.

3. Nursery Workers. They are vital because young parents will select a church more on the nursery care than on the doctrinal statements of the congregation. Nursery workers give assurance to the parents that their child will be cared for.

4. Greeters. They welcome people with a smile and a handshake. They are the ones who personally escort visitors to the appropriate rooms. They watch for people who appear lost or hunting for the right place. They look for the newcomers next week and greet them again.

5. The Persons Who Sit Next to a New Person in the Service. They help create a warm atmosphere when they smile and introduce themselves. They offer assistance by helping them locate a song, handing them a welcome card, or by sharing a Bible. They extend the church's hospitality by inviting them to a Sunday School class or a small group.

6. The Person Who Leads the Service. This individual spends a few moments greeting the people at the beginning or

during the service. This person must be warm, person-
able, positive, and real.

7. The Worship Leader. This person must also be friendly
   and have the ability to put people at ease.

8. The People Who Sing. Do they smile and look as if they
   enjoy what is going on?

9. The Pastor. He, too, must convey warmth and a sincere
   interest in people.

10. The Follow-up Person. This person must show apprecia-
    tion for the newcomers' visit and give a gracious invitation
    to return.

> —John C. Maxwell, *Ushers and Greeters* (El Cajon, Calif.: INJOY
> Ministries, 1991), 1–5.

Guests prefer the aisle seats and the seats in the rear of the
auditorium because these seats allow them to protect their
intimate space. However, that's the exact place most regular
attenders like to sit! If you want to guesterize your church, I
suggest you reserve the aisle seats and the rear seats for guests.
Encourage your regular attenders to sit in the middle of longer
rows and leave the best seats for guests.

Give Guests the Best Time

At the end of one church service, the pastor gave the
benediction, then reminded everyone, "Remember the Five-
Minute Rule." This intrigued me because I had never heard
of a five-minute rule. I later found out that the people of that
church had been instructed to speak to guests during the first
five minutes after each worship service. They were not to do
any church business or talk to their friends until five minutes
had elapsed. If you want to be a friendly church, I suggest you
reserve the first five minutes following every worship service
for your guests.

Give Guests the Best Service

Recently I visited a rather large church in southern California. As my wife and I stepped up on the curb to enter the front door, a woman greeted us by saying, "Hi! Is this your first time with us?" After we replied in a positive manner, she introduced herself, asked our names, and walked with us into the building to a welcome center. At the welcome center she introduced us by name to the person at the desk, who immediately offered help and gave us directions to important areas of the church such as the restrooms and the auditorium. As we were about to finish our conversation at the welcome center an usher walked up, and the person behind the desk introduced us by name to him. He then led us to our seats in the auditorium.

In just a few short minutes we had been introduced to several very friendly people, had our names mentioned three times, and been given all the initial information we needed. While you may not follow this church's exact procedure, if you want to guesterize your church, I suggest you follow the three principles they used:

- Approach new people promptly.
- Offer help and information.
- Introduce them by name to others.

Additionally, churches that serve their guests well typically use the following:

Parking Attendants. These workers do more than help guests find a good parking place. Most importantly, they offer a friendly greeting, a warm smile, and some give directions.

Greeters. Selected for their outgoing and friendly personality, these people should meet guests just outside the church building in warm weather and just inside the building in cold weather. Their prime role is to break the ice with newer guests and walk with them into the church building to the welcome table. Drop the word *greeters*. Replace it with the word *hosts*.

The implication of the term will help those who welcome guests to realize that their responsibility does not begin and end with a smile and a handshake.

Welcome Table. A welcome table should be hosted by people who express appreciation for the new person. These people must know the answers to everything a new person might ask. The most frequently asked questions are "Where are the restrooms?" " Where is the sanctuary?" and "Where do the children go?" Information about your church and all ministries should be available at this table in brochure form.

Ushers. Ushers are responsible for the comfort and care of guests once they enter the worship area. Above all, they should be friendly and not shy. They should give people a program and any information a new person may need to know about the worship service.

Pulpit Welcome. First-time guests often feel uneasy attending a church's worship service. The role of the pastor or person giving a welcome from the pulpit is mainly to put the new person at ease. Guests should be welcomed and encouraged to relax and enjoy the worship service. Be sure to tell guests that the offering is for members only. Advise new people of any information or irregularities about worship in your church. Remember: Don't embarrass them.

Refreshment Table. Most guests are quick to leave the sanctuary and church building after the worship service. To encourage them to stay longer, offer a refreshment table with coffee, juice, and light snacks. When people have a cup of coffee in one hand and a donut in the other, they typically will stay around until they finish their refreshment. It's best if the refreshment table can be located immediately outside the sanctuary or in the back where guests must pass by it on their way out of the church.

Introducers. These people are outgoing, friendly, and warm just like the greeters and ushers. The difference is they are responsible for not only meeting new guests but for introducing them to at least one other person in your church. While this can take place anywhere in the church, they should position themselves around the refreshment table, as it offers opportunities to meet and talk in a relaxed atmosphere.

Everyone a Greeter

Everyone in your church should be a greeter. Or a better way to put it is everyone in your church should be willing to serve others. A pastor told me how he accomplished this in one church. He began by mailing a letter to one-fourth of his regular worshipers asking them to pay special attention to new guests attending their church on the first Sunday of the month. The next week he mailed a similar letter to another fourth of his congregation asking them to welcome guests on the second Sunday of the month. He did this for another fourth of the congregation on the third Sunday and another fourth on the fourth Sunday.

In the following months he mailed a postcard to the same people with a friendly reminder that the next Sunday was their Sunday to greet guests. This took place for an entire year. Several months into this process, a lady approached the pastor commenting, "Pastor, it wasn't even my Sunday to greet people and I found myself doing it." This happened with many people. It created an interest in and awareness of welcoming guests to church.

In addition to greeting others, every member of your church should have the authority to help people solve their problems. My son worked for a home improvement store that gave superior service to its customers. If customers approached him and asked where to find an item, he was not allowed to point out the direction to them. Instead of giving directions, he was empowered to take them to the place where the item was located. Years ago when our children were babies, my wife and I visited Community Bible Church. Upon entering the building and being greeted, two people walked us to the nursery. After introducing us to the nursery workers and taking care of our children, they then took us to their Sunday School class and sat with us. We've never forgotten that church and have often recommended it to others. They guesterized in a way that met our needs, and we've told their story ever since.

Guesterizing a Church—A Summary

♦   Guesterizing a church means to make it more responsive to its guests and better able to attract new ones.

♦   To guesterize a church you should do the following:
   Give guests the best attitude.
   Give guests the best communication.
   Give guests the best welcome.
   Give guests the best parking.
   Give guests the best seating.
   Give guests the best time.
   Give guests the best service.

♦   The following ingredients are most often used effectively by churches to welcome their guests:
   parking attendants
   greeters (hosts)
   welcome table
   ushers
   pulpit welcome
   refreshment table
   introducers

- ◆ Encourage every worshiper to be a greeter by asking one-fourth of your congregation to be responsible to welcome newcomers one Sunday each month.
- ◆ Encourage worshipers to not simply give directions but to go the extra mile by taking people where they want to go.

____

Something to Think About

Being friendly accounts for only about 20 percent of a church's effectiveness in welcoming guests. The other 80 percent comes from well-designed systems.

____

Check It Out

Put a check mark (✔)in the appropriate column below

	We Have	We Don't Have
Parking attendants		
Greeters (Hosts)		
Welcome table		
Welcome table host		
Ushers		
Pulpit Greeting		
Refreshment table		
Introducers		

How to Get Good at Guesterizing

1. Rehearse the principles of guesterizing until you have them memorized.

2. Teach the principles to your leaders asking them to evaluate your church's success at fulfilling each one.

3. Review one principle each month.

4. Teach your worshipers the Five-Minute Rule and use it.

5. Teach your worshipers the "Ten-Foot Rule" and the "Just-Say-Hi" policy and use them.

6. Assemble a task force of people who have been in your church less than one year and ask them to design a new system for welcoming guests.

_____

CHAPTER ELEVEN

Follow Up Guests Appropriately

As church leaders, we understand that effective follow-up of guests is an important ingredient to our church's growth. Traditionally, churches have followed up guests through a personal visit in the new person's home by a pastor or calling team. Today many churches are finding that this method is not so effective as it used to be.

A new revolution of church ministry is taking place that is not likely to stop anytime soon. All aspects of church ministry need rethinking, and this includes what we call visitor follow-up. Church ministry is changing more than it has in the last few hundred years. In our unusually faddish era, ministries come and go. Programs that worked a few years ago may not work well today.

At best, a newly designed ministry has an effective life span of about three to five years. After that it will need to be revamped or, in some cases, scrapped for an entirely new approach. What remains constant during this period of rapid change is our relationship with people. Churches that hope to maintain loyalty focus on serving their people well. Such superior service includes excellent follow-up of our guests.

Suspects or Prospects

We make a mistake if we think of all guests as being the same. Guests may be divided into at least two groups: suspects and prospects. *Suspects* are guests who visit our church, and we suspect that they might be interested in the things of the Lord. *Prospects* are guests who attend our church, and we know for certain that they are interested in spiritual things.

This differentiation first dawned on me when I was a salesman in a home furnishings store. Being on commission, it didn't make sense to spend time with people who were just window shopping (suspects). Thus, I became adept at picking out the shoppers who were going to buy. It really is quite easy. If a man walks into a store and he has a checkbook in his back pocket, he is most likely a prospect. A woman who comes into a store carrying the store's recent ad from the newspaper is certainly a prospect.

A salesman's income depends on being able to spot and serve the prospects rather than the suspects. An effective follow-up plan depends on being able to separate the suspects from the true prospects who visit our worship service. Suspects are visitors who appear to be interested in Christ and the church, but are actually just looking. Prospects are people who are sincerely interested in Christ and the church.

In general, first-time guests are suspects. They may be interested in the Lord. They may be interested in the church. Yet, then again, maybe not. Guests who return for additional visits are the prospects. By attending your church again, they are in effect saying that they liked what they found the first time. They are back for a closer look.

Five Principles of Follow-Up

Visitor follow-up is most effective when visitors receive the following:

1. A Friendly Contact. Offer your friendship. Care should be taken not to offend new people.

2. A Personal Contact. Focus on the guest's interests and needs. Nothing takes the place of personal touch in our high-tech/high-touch age.

3. A Prompt Contact. Contact guests within twenty-four hours. The longer the time between their visit and a contact, the less effective the results.

4. A Nonthreatening Contact. Put the guest at ease. Guests have a natural uneasiness about new places and people.

5. A Continual Contact. Follow-up is a process, not an event. A one-time contact is not enough to be effective in our present environment.

A Four-Step Plan

The most effective retention of visitors occurs when follow-up focuses on prospects rather than suspects. Church growth studies have found that the average church in the United States keeps 16 percent of all first-time guests. In contrast, the average church keeps 85 percent of its second-time guests!

Effective retention of guests occurs when follow-up focuses on building relationships. Many churches use an institutional approach to follow-up. They focus on what the church needs rather than on caring for the guest. It is important for guests to perceive that the church is interested in them and their needs.

Today's guests want their visit acknowledged but are not expecting a visit from the pastor. Churches located in cities, high-tech and crime-ridden areas will find that people do not want someone showing up on their doorstep without an appointment. Non-Christians and those who find the church threatening wish to remain somewhat anonymous, but not ignored.

Step 1: Acknowledgment

The day following guests' first visit to your church a call should be made thanking them for attending your services. Use a person with a friendly phone voice. Shut-ins or the elderly may find this a place for ministry. Call Sunday afternoon if possible, but no later than Monday evening.

Calling all guests within a twenty-four- to forty-eight-hour time period shows you care about them and begins to cement your relationship with them. Surveys among businesses found that customers who are called rank the company's service 20 percent higher than those who aren't called.[1] A phone call is received as well as a personal visit in most cases.

If they have time, another excellent way to communicate your desire to serve your guests and find out important information is to interview them over the phone. Present your interview in such a way that your guests can ignore it if they don't want to participate. Always ask politely and never force them to answer.

When they do answer, listen to their words; but more important, listen to the tone of their voice and what they *don't* say. Learn to read between the lines and you'll improve your church's follow-up. Listening is not just hearing. It's understanding. What do our guests think about us? (See the sample phone interview in this chapter.)

The conversation doesn't need to be long. Just be sure to do two things. First, thank them for visiting your church. Second, invite them back! If they are open to talking, ask, "How may we help you?" Find out why they visited your church.

Ask open-ended questions to further understand their needs. Then, do all that you can to meet their needs. Open-ended questions call for information. They contain words like *who, what, where, why,* and *how.* Most importantly, open-ended questions will not only help you understand people, but they demonstrate your concern and care for their needs. When a phone call is followed up with a personal letter, about 50 percent of those contacted will return to your church for another visit.

Most churches send a personal letter to newcomers thanking them for attending church. Further information about the church is often enclosed along with times of services, ministries of interest, and special events. A good letter thanks the guests for attending, outlines the times of services, offers general help, and is signed by the senior pastor.

This letter could be made even more useful by enclosing a short questionnaire similar to the one that follows.

We'd Like to Know . . .

1. What did you enjoy most about attending our church?

_____

_____

_____

2. If you could have changed one thing during your visit, what would it have been? _____

_____

_____

3. How could our church have served your needs more
completely? _____

_____

_____

Thank You Very Much
(Your Church Name)
(Church Logo)
(Church Slogan)

It could be a simple, pre-stamped reply card that could
be returned in the mail. While it is important to get the
information, it is even more important to underscore the fact
that your church really cares about its guests. Asking for their
opinion is a good way to point it out without actually making
the statement.

Place them on your church mailing list. Use a general
mailing list for all potential contacts and a prime list for all
regular attenders. Mail brochures, church newsletters, and
general information to people on the general mailing list.
Remember: The purpose of this first step is to get the guest
to return for a second visit.

Step 2: Appointment

After making the phone call and mailing the letter, wait
until the newcomer makes a second visit to your church. By
waiting for them to visit once again, you are allowing them to
determine if they are a suspect or a prospect. Those who do
not return were just suspects, and it is good that you didn't
spend too much energy focusing on them at this time. Those
who return for a second visit are your real prospects and are
the people to whom you need to give your attention.

The week following the guest's second visit to your
church, call them and ask for an appointment. Depending on

the demographics of your community, as many as nine out of ten will typically prefer not to meet with you. If they say no to your request, that is fine. Give them the space and time they need to feel comfortable at your church. For those who say no, ask if you may mail them further information concerning your church. If they say yes, schedule an appointment. Don't limit your thinking to evening appointments only. A breakfast or luncheon appointment at a local restaurant may be received better than asking for a visit in their home. You could also invite them to your home after church. In most cases in today's environment it is unwise to show up at their home unexpectedly. People will feel pressured into inviting you inside their home. If they have not had the time to prepare for your visit and feel embarrassed by the condition of their home, they may not return to your church.

Mail further information about your church and its ministries to them. Develop a detailed information piece on your church. This should be different than what was mailed after the first visit and should provide additional information about your church. Since they have returned for a second visit, you should assume they want to know more about your church. Be prepared to provide detailed information about every ministry. A small brochure for each ministry would be good to have on hand.

Step 3: Enhancement

The week following the third visit to your church, alert the guests that you know they were visiting again. A greeting card or specially designed postcard works well. It is important at this point to let them know that your church has something of value to offer them in terms of their interests or needs.

You can expect that four out of five guests who visit your church three times without finding what they're looking for won't return. Arrange a second phone call or visit from someone in the church who has similar interests or may be able to meet their needs. If they are interested in crafts, sports, or a hobby, have someone who has like interests call the guest.

Phone Questionnaire for Visitors

Hello, I'm _____ from _____ Church. Is this
_____ ?

I understand you attended our service Sunday (date).

I'm sorry I didn't get a chance to meet you, but I want to thank you for coming. Perhaps next time I'll get a chance to meet you. Do you have the time to help me by giving your opinions on a few questions about the church?

_ [Yes]? Great. [Go to survey]

– [No]? When would be a good time for me to call back? (date and time) I'll be looking forward to talking to you then.

1. Did you have difficulty locating our church?
_ Yes. What was most difficult?_____

_____

_ No. [Go to next question (GNQ)]

2. Did you have difficulty finding parking?
_ Yes. What was most difficult?_____

_____

_ No. [GNQ]

3. Were you greeted before the service?
_ Yes.
_ No.

4. Did you enter from the street or parking lot?_____

_____

5. Did you receive adequate directions prior to the service to meet your needs?

_ Yes.

– No. What directions did you need?_____

_____

6. Did you have any problems finding a seat?

_ Yes. What happened?_____

_____

_ No. [GNQ]

7. Did you feel welcome?

_ Yes. What made you feel welcome?_____

_____

_ No. What made you feel unwelcome?_____

_____

8. What did you like most about the service?_____

_____

9. What suggestions could you give us to improve the service?_____

_____

10. How did you learn about our church?_____

_____

11. Do you plan to attend our church again in the near future?

_ Yes.

_ No.

12. Do you regularly attend church anywhere?

_ Yes.

_ No.

13. Would you like to know more about our church?
_Yes. What would you like to know?_____

_____

_____

_____

— No. OK
I appreciate your willingness to help us out by answering these questions. You've been a big help. Thank you very much.

Additional Comments

_____

_____

_____

_____

_____

A creative way to enhance service to your guests is the employment of a "Candy Express" team. Once guests have visited your church a third time, send out a team of people to visit their home. The team's purpose is not to visit in the home but to leave a gift of candy (Candy Express), cookies (Cookie Express), flowers (Flower Express), or baked bread (Bread Express).

In no case are the members of the team to go into the home, even if invited. They leave the gift as a further thank-you for attending your church. This extra special thank-you creates good rumors about your church and lets the guests know they are appreciated. In communities where people may be wary of accepting homemade gifts like baked bread, use wrapped packages of candy or cookies purchased from a local store. The gift doesn't need to be expensive, but a cheap gift is not received well either. The point is to do something that the guest doesn't expect. By surprising your guests with an extra special touch, you not only increase the chance they'll come back, but you provide them with a positive story to share by word of mouth to their friends.

Step 4: Commitment

The week immediately following the guest's fourth visit to your church, ask for modest commitment to your church. Say, "We've noticed you have been attending on a regular basis. Would you like your name placed in our directory?" This assumes you have a directory that can be changed once every three months. Pictorial directories are not good for this. A computerized directory that can be updated and printed every three months works very well, however. Placing new-comers' names in your directory does not overcommit them to your church; nor does it make them a member. What it does do is help them identify with your church in a small way. It helps them begin to think, "This is my church."

If they are non-Christians or new believers, invite them to a new believers class for orientation to the Christian faith. It is best to use a creative name for the class rather than calling it a new believers class. Try a name like "Understanding What You Believe." The class should teach on topics like salvation, assurance of salvation, and basic Bible doctrines. If they are already Christians, invite them to a new members class for orientation to your church. Once again, a different name for the class is best. A name such as "How to Belong" or "Getting to Know First Baptist" is good. The purpose of this class should be to introduce your church—your purpose, values, philosophy—to the newcomer. Nine out of ten people who take this class will become members or regular worshipers in your church.

Many guests will have irregular patterns of attendance. Follow the process outlined above whenever the guest returns within six months. If it is longer than six months, start over from the beginning and follow through to the end.

By following the above plan, you will contact the guest up to eight times in four weeks. These recurring contacts will build a relationship that will lead to possible commitment. Churches that use plans like this often retain nearly 25 percent of their first-time visitors.

We shouldn't assume anything. In the final analysis it doesn't make any difference how we think guests should be greeted. What matters is what the guest wants. The only way to know for sure is to ask them what they want. There are several ways to do this.

Your church should survey your neighborhood in person or by phone. This has become popular with church planters as a means to discover what nonchurch attenders want from a church. It usually involves just a few questions like these.

1. Do you attend any church?

   _ Yes. Thank you for your help. Please have a nice day.

   _ No. (Go to next question.)

2. If you were to attend church, what would you look for?

3. Why don't you attend church?

4. Would you be interested in receiving information from a church that would be like you described?

We don't need to be church planters to survey the people in our community. What's important is that you get information that helps you understand people's needs. Asking potential guests what they want in a church will help you design a follow-up process that works in your community.

Following Up Guests—A Summary

♦ Follow-up of guests is an important part of a church's growth mix. Traditional forms of follow-up such as a letter and personal visit to the home are not working as well today as they once have, however.

♦ Two types of guests visit a church: suspects and prospects. People who attend a church one time are usually suspects, but those who attend two or more times are genuine prospects.

♦ The most effective retention of guests occurs when follow-up focuses on second-time guests, building relationships, and meeting the expectations of guests.

♦ Following up guests is best defined by a process rather than an event. A suggested four-step approach is:

    Step 1: Acknowledgment
    Step 2: Appointment
    Step 3: Enhancement
    Step 4: Commitment

Something to Think About

The last impression your guests have of your church will stay with them until they return again—if they ever do.

Do You Know How You're Doing?

How effective is your present system of follow-up? Find out by filling in the following blanks:

1. A total of _____ first-time guests visited our church during the past twelve months. (Count only those people who live in your ministry area.)

2. A total of _____ new people became members or regular worshipers during the same twelve months.

3. Dividing the answer in question #2 by that in #1 equals _____ percent.

4. Based on this percentage, circle the category of effective follow-up below.

0% to 8% POOR
9% to 13% FAIR

14% to 18% AVERAGE
19% to 24% GOOD
25% or more EXCELLENT

What category of follow-up effectiveness does your church fall into? _____

Where would you like it to be? _____

What can you begin to do right now to make it better?

_____

_____

Room for Improvement

There is always room for improvement in your follow-up plan. Look over the suggested steps and determine where you can improve.

Step 1: Acknowledgment

♦ We call guests within forty-eight hours.

♦ We send a thank-you letter within two days.

♦ We ask guests for their opinions through a phone interview or a written questionnaire.

♦ We place all first-time guests on our mailing list.

♦ We do all we can to get first-time guests to return a second time.

Step 2: Appointment

♦ We call to make an appointment with guests who visit us two or more times.

♦ We schedule appointments for breakfast and lunch rather than just in people's homes during the evening.

♦ We have a special brochure of each ministry our church offers which we can send to our guests.

♦ We are sensitive to our guests and allow them to take their time getting acquainted with our church.

Step 3: Enhancement

♦ We let guests know we appreciate them by using a specially designed postcard or note card mailed to their home following their third visit to our church.

♦ We try to meet our guests' needs and interests by directing them to specific people or ministries they would find helpful.

♦ We give them extra service by delivering a special gift to their home.

Step 4: Commitment

♦ We ask guests if they would like to put their names in our church directory.

♦ We invite guests who have visited our church four times to participate in a new believers class or a new members class.

CHAPTER TWELVE

Build Pathways of Belonging

A number of years ago I accepted a position at a company which did a very good job of welcoming its new employees. The night before my first day on the job, I was so nervous I woke up several times and did not get much sleep. When I arrived at my new place of employment, I was met warmly at the reception desk by the vice-president of the company who personally escorted me to my office. He told me to take about thirty minutes to get settled, put a few things in my desk, and then to meet him in his office. When I was finished, I went to his office, where he was waiting for me. He then proceeded to take me on a walking tour of the entire facility. Along the way he introduced me to every employee from management to the mail room. He answered any questions that I asked and generally gave me a superb introduction to the company. We went to lunch with the president and two additional vice-presidents of the company. During lunch they casually shared their basic values and philosophies of work. My entire first day was given to meeting people and getting acquainted with the company. Nothing was even discussed about my particular job assignment until the second day.

What took place on my first day on the job was what should take place in every church that has a culture of service. The vice-president who led me throughout the day was building pathways of belonging for me. Churches should do the same for their guests.

Pathways that Your Church Can Build

Pathways are strategically designed ministries which assist new people to gain ownership in your church. In a broad sense, building pathways has been the focus of this entire book. Recognizing that people outside of our church are living without salvation in Jesus Christ, we have been building a culture of service that helps them walk along a pathway which leads to Christ. The pathway leads from their first becoming aware of your church, to their initial visit, to being served well through your various ministries, to involvement in your church. At this point we are thinking of building pathways within your church that will assist new people to understand your church, meet people, and become involved.

There are, of course, many pathways of belonging. Some happen without much planning. A new person meets someone at your church and they discover a common kinship which draws them together. I saw this take place once when a new person who was visiting my church met another man and they began talking about their love—computers. From that point on, it was quite common to find both of them together discussing some aspects of bits and bytes of computers that the rest of us could barely decipher. A pathway of belonging had developed quite naturally.

What we are talking about in this chapter are pathways that have been developed intentionally to lead people into ownership of our church's culture. This means helping them understand what our church is all about—our mission, values, plans, and goals.

Staff Reception

In the early stages a staff reception for new guests helps people gain some knowledge of the church and staff. In smaller churches a staff reception can be offered once a month, while in larger churches it could be a regular Sunday morning event. A room is set aside in the church where new guests may come for light refreshments and to meet the pastor or pastoral staff. An invitation is extended from the pulpit, in the program, and by greeters and others who meet guests throughout the morning. The staff reception is designed to give new people an initial acquaintance with the leaders of the church. The atmosphere should be warm and welcoming with casual conversation. No teaching or lecturing takes place. Newcomers come and go as they desire.

The Pastor's Dessert

A good beginning on the pathway to belonging is for your church to host a pastor's dessert. The pastor of your church begins by reserving one night a month for this dessert. For sake of illustration, let's say your pastor designates the third Tuesday of every month for the dessert. The dessert may be held at a home or at the church facility. It begins between 7:00 P.M. and 7:30 P.M., giving people time to arrive home from work, eat, and relax for a little while.

The purpose of the pastor's dessert is to welcome those who have attended the church a minimum of three times. Thus, attendance is by invitation only. No announcements or invitations are given publicly. Instead, a nicely printed invitation, similar to a wedding invitation, is mailed to each person who has been identified as visiting at least three times. Guests R.S.V.P., and the dress is casual.

A friendly welcome is extended as people arrive and refreshments are served. As people finish their dessert, the pastor welcomes everyone. He briefly introduces the mission of the church, its key values and larger vision for the future. He then formally introduces the rest of the staff and/or other church leaders. In a small church all leaders may be at the dessert, but in most cases only a few selected leaders will be present. After introducing the staff, the pastor then asks each person present to introduce himself and tell how they first heard about the church.

Questions and answers are given as time permits and if people show an interest. Someone should take careful note of the ways new people say they heard of the church. These statements will let you know how well your ads, mailings, and word-of-mouth advertising is working. The pastor ends the dessert with a personal invitation to attend the orientation class.

Orientation Class

My son went to work for a home improvement company and his first two weeks on the job were spent attending an orientation course. He was given a copy of the company's policy manual and for two weeks was instructed in the culture of that company. He was told not only the policies of the company, which we might expect, but more importantly was instructed in the attitudes and actions the company expected from its employees in serving its customers.

We need to have an orientation course in our churches also. Throughout the years, churches have offered a new members class. In former years if people wanted to be members, a new members class told them how to do so. Instructions were given on the differences in denominations, and the church's bylaws were reviewed with special emphases on the section having to do with church membership. The class assisted people who came from a different denomination to understand the new church and its polity. In most instances, if persons came from the same denomination, they bypassed the class.

There continues to be a need for this type of class but with some changes. The purpose of an orientation class is to introduce people to your church culture. This means that all new people are expected to attend, even those who come from a sister church or one of like faith. Your church polity and history may be the same as that of other churches in your denomination, but your church's culture will likely be very different. Since the purpose of this class is to orientate people to your church's culture, everyone must attend. An orientation class helps people accept your church culture from the beginning. Giving people an in-depth look at your church lets them make a well-informed decision about whether or not this is the church for them. It may also promote rejection, which is important. Some people, having heard your philosophy of ministry may decide this is not the church for them. Whatever, people ultimately make a decision about staying, everyone hears the same message, and they get started off on the right foot.

The pastor must be the teacher of this class in small churches, but in larger ones a staff member can do the job following the senior pastor's invitation at the dessert. Since people in our era are not particularly drawn to a church for membership, it is good not to name the class a "new members class." Find a name that communicates a different value such as "Meet Hope Community Church" or "How to Belong." Churches find that four to six hours is enough to get the job done. An orientation class offered on a Saturday morning or afternoon or perhaps in four to six weeks on Sunday morning works well. Experiment with different time schedules until you find what works best for your people. Some of the topics to be included should be

- a brief history of your church, highlighting your core values;
- a review of your church's mission or purpose statement;
- a review of your church's philosophy of ministry;
- a review of your church's vision and goals for ministry;
- time spent in small group discussion to get acquainted with each other and form new friendships;
- introductions to the various ministries and how people may serve others through them;
- introductions to selected ministry leaders;
- information on the next steps to get involved, including how to become a member.

First impressions are lasting, so take extra special care to make this class an exciting introduction to your church. It should be fun! Take the class on a tour of the church facilities and make sure they meet the main staff. Once or twice during the class host a party at someone's home or at a local restaurant. Instead of lecturing all the time, use small groups to help the new people get to know each other and discover the values, philosophies, and their role in your church together.

Throughout the class, refer to your church as "our church." If a person begins a question with "Your church . . ." correct her and have them start over saying, "*Our* church . . ." Help them gain ownership from day one.

Small Groups

Gaining ownership in a church takes place as people make friends and participate in a class or group. Both of these things can take place together, and a good way to facilitate it is to extend the orientation class into a small group. If you use small groups in the orientation class, it often works well to move the class into a small group or Sunday School class format. New people find it easiest to make friends with other new people. They may develop beginning friendships in your class which they will want to continue rather than dropping the class. Ask the class if they would enjoy continuing on together as a small group meeting on an evening or on Sunday mornings as their own class? If they desire to do one or the other, you will have established a new class or group and further assisted the new people to gain ownership in your church.

Dinner Eights

It may be that the new people will not want to continue the orientation class as a small group or Sunday School class. In that case, you need to be ready to help them move down some additional pathways of belonging. One process that has worked well is what has been termed Dinner Eights or Dinner Sixes. Briefly, a new couple or individual agrees to alternate hosting a meal at their home with two or three other couples or individuals. Once each month for three or four months, the group moves from one home to another for a meal. The purpose of the meals is to get to know each other better.

In a smaller church, it often works well to have the pastor or another church leader be one of the couples or individuals along with a new family and a regular church member. This helps the new family get to know church members and feel like they are a part of the church. It's always best if groups can be formed from people with similar interests.

New Believers Class

There will be some new people who need teaching in the basic doctrines of your church and the Christian faith. Thus, a new believers class is another pathway for some people to follow. The purpose of this class is to teach people the basics of salvation, assurance of salvation, and other beginning aspects of being a disciple of Jesus Christ. This class also serves to explain the differences in church distinctives that some may have an interest in learning about. Some will not need this class, therefore it usually is not required of every new person but only those who are new to the Christian faith or have unanswered questions. Participation in this class should be by invitation publicly and privately.

Placement Interview

A key aspect often found in a church with a culture of service is the ability to involve people in a place of service. The most successful way to recruit new people is through a personal interview process. The orientation class will have introduced people to your church's various ministries. Some new people may have taken the initiative to become involved in a ministry on their own. For those who have not, an interview should be scheduled where their gifts, talents, previous experience, and ministry desires are discovered. Following the interview, a ministry counselor from your church should offer several possibilities of ministry and put them in touch with the director of the ministries they select. A concerted effort to interview and place new people will pay rich dividends. New people are the easiest to recruit since they come into your church with a sense of excitement and a willingness to serve. Does anyone ever join a church with a bad attitude? Well, there are occasionally bad transfers, but in most cases, people who join your church have great attitudes about your church and want to be involved in ministry.

Caring for Others

The London Observer reported a few years ago that a platoon of Chinese soldiers were stationed at a little place called Quingsha in the heart of the Gobi Desert. Their only job was to keep the railroad track clear of blowing sand. No passengers travel by train along the track to Quingsha except for an occasional soldier. The only freight the railroad carries are supplies for the soldiers stationed there. The soldiers' only orders are to maintain the railroad track, and the railroad's only function is to supply the soldiers. Sounds like some churches who, having forgotten their primary mission, spend all their energy caring only for themselves.[1]

In a culture of service, we spend more time caring for others than for ourselves. This means, among other things, that we must build pathways of belonging for the new people coming our way. What can you do to cause your guests to become involved in your church? What pathways are available now that new people may follow to establish ownership in your church? When you answer these questions carefully and then follow them up with action, you'll find that people develop a loyalty to your church and your culture of service.

Pathways of Belonging—A Summary

♦ Pathways are strategically designed ministries which assist new people to gain ownership in your church.

♦ Staff Receptions allow new guests to gain introductory information and meet the pastor and church staff.

♦ A Pastor's Dessert extends a warm welcome to guests who have attended your church at least three times.

♦ An Orientation Class provides in-depth exposure to all aspects of your church culture.

♦ Small Groups offer new people a place to make friends and belong.

♦ Dinner Eights is another way to help new people meet others and make new friends.

♦ A New Believers Class teaches new believers and people from other churches the basics of the Christian faith, as well as explaining differences in church distinctives.

♦ A Placement Interview moves new people toward finding a place of ministry in your church.

Something to Think About

The various pathways to belonging help people accept your church's ministry and, just as importantly, help some people reject it.

The Worst Welcome

Here's a fun activity that helps newcomers express themselves and alerts you to dangers you can avoid.

In your next orientation class, divide the class members into three or more groups. Ask them to think of the worst experience they can remember when first visiting a church. Have them select one case, embellish it, making it as ugly as can be.

They then act out the skit in a fun sort of way. They get to vent their frustration, and you get to see what not to do in your church. Once they all finish, ask them to return to their groups and remake the story into a positive one, improving on it in any way possible. Then they perform the good experience in skits.

When they are done, tell them you want your church to be like the good skits. Ask them to help you make your church a place where people have good experiences, not poor ones.

Exit Statement

Mission or purpose statements are found commonly in churches. It is also a good idea to write an "exit statement."

Visualize an impartial person standing outside your church asking each person who leaves this question: "How would you describe the treatment you just experienced in this church?"

Write down exactly what you hope their responses would be.

Insight: If you want your guests to feel a certain way after leaving, you can insure that feeling by the treatment you give them when they're with you.

PART FIVE

Empowering a Culture of Service

CHAPTER THIRTEEN

Empower Your Strategy

A few months ago I was shopping for some binoculars for my son. At one store I asked to see a small pair which could be placed in the glove compartment of a car quite easily. The binoculars were square in shape, and when I placed them to my eyes, I inadvertently looked through the wrong end. Looking through them was like peering down a long tunnel. Only after turning them around was I able to see correctly.

Like looking in the wrong end of binoculars, church leaders often take a narrow view of service and hence a narrow view of how to produce it. As you have seen in previous chapters, creating a culture of service in a church is a big concept. It involves many areas of church ministry. Thus, we must take a broader view of the issue and cast off our tunnel vision.

Where to Start

When I was growing up, one of my favorite television programs was sponsored by Borax detergent. The picture

on the box was of twenty mules pulling wagons out of a
borax pit in California in the 1880s. Twenty Mule Team
Borax was a household name for many years. The origina-
tion of the twenty-mule team is an interesting story. Origi-
nally, one wagon was pulled by twelve mules. Then
someone began experimenting with different combinations
of mules and wagons and discovered that by adding an
additional eight mules to the team, the twenty could then
pull two wagons of borax and one small water wagon.
Therefore, by working together fewer mules could pull a
greater load and accomplish more work.

Four Factors to Building a Culture of Service

A culture of service becomes more powerful as each aspect
is added. All the elements we've looked at so far work together.
The more elements which are in place, the more they pull a
church toward excellent service to all people. It should be
obvious that everything cannot be done at once. Planning and
prioritizing are the keys to building a culture of service. What
aspects to implement first depends on four factors.

Your church's basic health. Is your church growing, pla-
teaued, or declining? An unhealthy church will find that it
cannot develop a culture of service until some basic problems
are dealt with. Sick churches cannot afford to develop a
culture of service because they are too tied up dealing with
internal needs and problems to serve others. So the first step
in planning for a new culture of service is to evaluate your
church's health.[1]

Your position in your community. Do you have a good
reputation or a poor one? Do you have good visibility or poor
visibility? A surprisingly accurate thermometer of church
reputation is word of mouth, as indicated by the attitudes and
satisfaction level of people who have visited your church. If
good research and surveys of people indicate that your church

has a poor reputation for service, then you probably need to work on basic issues before your even begin. Stop now. Don't injure your church and your ministry by pushing for dramatic changes in your church culture. Even though you may succeed in writing a new mission statement and other mechanical aspects of a new church culture, they'll end up being only a whitewash job that quickly flakes away, wasting your time and other resources of your church. Instead, concentrate on fixing the underlying problems and come back to installing a new culture of service after you've succeeded.

What elements are already strongly in place? Unless certain prerequisites or indispensable elements are firmly established, it is probably useless to start using them in a culture of service. A key element in developing a culture of service is common sense. Don't institute new changes so quickly that the entire church is destroyed. It is pointless to launch a new culture of service unless the leadership of your church is committed to it. Heading into a new direction and then losing interest does more harm than good. It's folly to begin beating the drum of sacrificial service unless your leaders understand the cost and are willing to pay the price to see it through.

What you can do quickly (with little effort) and what will take longer. The best way to start is by achieving some early, easy, and inexpensive victories. These early wins demonstrate ways in which your culture of service can be developed. Many things can be done. One of them is for leaders to begin fostering a culture of service by changing their own behavior—giving up special parking spaces, handing out their home phone numbers, praising those who demonstrate superior service to others. In general, expect a long campaign to implement the elements of superior service. In most churches you will be pushing profound changes in the overall way of thinking and acting. As mentioned earlier, cultures—especially strong ones—take years to change. Redesigning core programs and ministries to reflect a spirit of service cannot be done overnight.

Empowering a Culture of Service

An anonymous person supposedly quipped, "Adopting a philosophy ain't what gets things done." Adapting that statement we could conclude that "Adopting a culture of service ain't what gets things done." Just because we say we are going to put people first or serve people well isn't what accomplishes it. It gets done when we actually *do* an act of service. Changing a church's culture takes commitment, persistence, and time. People have to change and so does the infrastructure and systems that support them. Here's a simple look in principle form of what it takes to empower a culture of service in your church.

Principles of Empowerment

What gets pictured gets done. My wife loves to put together jigsaw puzzles. At holidays we often retrieve a puzzle from our garage, spread it out on a table, and the entire family works to put it together. One thing I've noticed is that it's easier to put the puzzle together when we first look at the picture on the box. I hate to think how long it would take to complete if we didn't have the picture. If you hope to empower a culture of service in your church, you must paint a verbal picture of what you want for your people. Find a story that illustrates the culture of service you want to build and tell that story over and over until it becomes legend. People lose the vision within about a month, so talk about your culture of service every chance you get.

I recently read a story about a man who coached his son's soccer team. After experiencing a number of losses, the father asked the team what he could do for them to help them win. They told him they sometimes got confused as to which goal was theirs. From that time on, the coach stood on the sidelines and pointed in the direction of their goal. Guess what? The team went undefeated the rest of the season. Our true role as leaders is to point people in the direction of the goal.

What gets modeled gets done. The most frightening verse in the Bible to me is "Be imitators of me, just as I also am of Christ" (1 Cor. 11:1). I used to think that Paul must have been arrogant to say such a thing. Now I know it's true of every leader, whether we want it to be or not. People do imitate their leaders. You can talk all you want about your new culture of service, but if people see you and other leaders in your church behaving in ways that don't support your talk, you will find you are powerless. People are boss-watchers, or in our case, leader-watchers. They conclude what is really important from what you do. Empowering a culture of service gains momentum as people see you and other church leaders actually modeling sacrificial service to others.

What gets praised gets done. People learn quickly what gets applauded and what does not get applauded in a church. If praise is given for cooking in the kitchen, or driving students to camp, or whatever, people will lean toward involvement in that area of ministry. Empowering a culture of service happens as you catch people serving others and reward them for doing it. Praise the behavior you want to reinforce. The behavior that is reinforced is the behavior that is repeated. The behavior that is repeated becomes the prevailing attitude. The prevailing attitude becomes your church's culture.

Keep the Vision Alive

When Michelangelo was a boy, one of his father's friends gave him a small Greek sculpture of a young man half chiseled out of marble. The base of the statue was a square block of stone with the marks of the chisel still upon it as it had been cut from the quarry. About half the way up from the base, the form emerged to take human shape. Michelangelo kept that little statue beside his bed. It was the last thing he saw before he went to sleep at night and the first thing he saw upon wakening. For him it spoke of beauty's anguished effort to be liberated from the ugly and plain. Michelangelo devoted his life to freeing figures from stone.

Beside my bed I keep a little Bible. It is the last thing I see when I go to sleep and the first thing I see upon wakening. It reminds me that our world is filled with people needing to be freed from their prisons of ignorance, self-destructive behavior, and alienation from God.

Most pastors have times of discouragement. They are tempted to give up. We ask, "What is the use?" when things seem never to change or to get worse. At such times, we need to remember that, like Michelangelo, nothing worthwhile was ever accomplished in a short time. The sculptor would sometimes work months or years to free a figure from its stony prison. The thing that kept him going was the vision of the man or woman locked up in the marble. In a similar way, we need to keep going, driven by the vision that there is a marriage that will be repaired, a life that will be salvaged, and an eternity that will be gained for someone imprisoned to sin and death.

—Dr. Jon H. Allen; used by permission, *Illustration Digest,*
P.O. Box 170, Winslow, AR 72959 (501)634-3434.

What gets trained gets done. Over the last thirty-three years I have worshiped and served in a number of churches. In all of them I was encouraged to use my gifts by serving in some area of ministry. In none of them was I trained to serve. I guess they all felt that, by some magical trick or spiritual insight, I would just know how to care for others or how to teach or how to counsel or how to share my faith. What little training I received came from para-church organizations or from secular schools and businesses which I then transferred into the realm of church ministry. Many of those churches were ineffective, partly because of their inability to train their members. Empowering a culture of service means you must teach people what is important in your church. The growth of a church is really the combined growth of its individuals.

People only do what they know how to do. If people are not serving each other well, ask yourself, "Do they know how to care for each other?" It is the leader's responsibility to train people so they know how to serve each other. Make certain they know your mission, values, and philosophy. Adults want to learn the philosophy behind the culture as well as the skills to carry it out. When you think about it, designing a culture of service is as much attitude as it is mechanics. Training really has to begin with philosophy. Train them how to welcome guests and give practical examples of ways to serve others. Offer classes where people may develop their listening skills. If you are unable to do the training yourself, at least take responsibility for bringing in trainers from outside your church to do it for you. But be sure of this: A church that cares for others and serves their needs is one that nurtures people in a learning environment.

What gets measured gets done. The only way we can ever really know if we reach our goals is to try to measure our progress. An old saying tells us, "What gets inspected gets done, not what is expected." Empowering a culture of service requires setting standards, then measuring results to see if they are matching up. For example, what percentage of first-time guests do you want to keep? How often do you plan on redecorating your facilities? How many training events will you sponsor this year? Make sure your people know your goals and then measure your results each year to see if you're reaching them. The key to long-term success is to keep setting your goals higher to keep your church moving forward. "Raise the bar," as high jumpers say. Constant improvement, even small improvements, is the only way to engineer a higher quality of service in your church.

What gets budgeted gets done. Anything worth doing takes resources—time, energy, people, money. For any plan to come to life, enough money must be designated to make it happen. Empowering a culture of service in your church means you will need to budget money for training, advertising, and upgrading your facilities. Each year graph your budget by major categories and observe where the most money is designated. Note where the least amount of money is spent. What priorities does your expenditure reflect? What do you want it to say? I estimate that most churches spend 15 percent of their money on things that they don't need to do. To find more money, ask yourself three burning questions about every ministry in your church: (1) "Why do we do this?" (2) "Do we need to do it at all?" (3) "Could we make better use of the resources we spend on it somewhere else?"

What Are You Building?

A popular story circulated among leaders is placed in the days of misty towers, distressed maidens, and stalwart knights. A young man, walking down a road, came upon a laborer fiercely pounding away at a stone with hammer and chisel. The laborer looked frustrated and angry. The lad asked the worker, "What are you doing?" The laborer answered, "I'm trying to shape this stone, and it's backbreaking work." The youth continued his journey and soon came upon another man chipping away at a similar stone, who looked neither particularly angry or happy. "What are you doing?" he asked. "I'm shaping a stone for a building," came the quick reply.

The young man went on and soon came to a third worker chipping away at a stone, but this worker was singing happily as he worked. "What are you doing?" The worker smiled and replied, "I'm building a cathedral."

It takes a great deal of work to engineer a new culture of service in a church. If you find yourself a pioneer, you likely will be the one with the arrows in your back. Keeping the proper perspective is a must. We are not just carving a stone, we are building a cathedral where sacrificial service will shine as Jesus intended it to.[2]

Getting Started—A Summary

♦   A culture of service takes shape as the ingredients discussed throughout this book are put into place. The more ingredients that are in place, the more a culture of service is developed.

♦   Four factors govern where a church begins:

1. The basic health of your church

2. The reputation of your church in your community

3. The commitment of your church leaders

4. The number of ministries which can be put into place quickly

♦   Empowering a culture of service is based on six key principles:

1. What gets pictured gets done

2. What gets modeled gets done

3. What gets praised gets done

4. What gets trained gets done

5. What gets measured gets done

6. What gets budgeted gets done

Something to Think About

You always get back what you give out.

How to Use These Ideas

Merely reading this book will do you little good. Knowing information, or having knowledge, is of little value until it finds its way into your church's actions.

Go back and read each chapter, making notes in the margin of the book, scribbling your thoughts and ideas.

Then make a list of action steps that you want your church to take during the next year to develop a culture of service.

Put your action steps on note cards and carry them with you. As each action step is accomplished, scratch it off your list. Read your list every day until all the action steps have been completed.

Assessing Your Empowerment

1. In what ways are you communicating your new culture of service to your people?_____

_____

2. In what ways are you modeling a culture of service to those who are watching you?_____

_____

3. What types of behaviors receive the praise in your church?_____

_____

What behaviors would you like to see praised?_____

_____

_____

4. What training has been conducted over the past year to help people learn how to serve others? What training could be done in the next year?_____

_____

_____

5. What goals do you have in place to help your church provide better service to others?_____

_____

_____

How do you plan on measuring your success?_____

_____

_____

6. What does your budget say about your priorities?___

_____

_____

What area of the budget must be changed to reflect your commitment to empower a new culture of service in your church?_____

_____

_____

Notes

Chapter 1

1. Those wishing to study the concept of corporate culture in depth should begin by reading Terrence E. Deal and Allan A. Kennedy, *Corporate Culture* (New York: Addison-Wesley Publishing Co., Inc., 1982).

2. Karl Albrecht, *The Only Thing that Matters* (New York: HarperBusiness, 1992), 95.

Chapter 4

1. Win Arn and Charles Arn, *Who Cares about Love?* (Pasadena: Church Growth Press, 1986).

Chapter 5

1. Ron Willingham, *Hey, I'm the Customer* (Englewood Cliffs, N.J.: Prentice Hall, 1992), 9,11.

Chapter 6

1. Cheryl Russell, "Editor's Note: Bad Service," *American Demographics,* November 1987, 7.

Chapter 7

1. Jerry R. Wilson, *Word-of-Mouth Marketing* (New York: John Wiley & Sons, Inc., 1991), 22.

2. Ibid.

Chapter 9

1. For an excellent up-to-date resource on starting new ministries, see Robert E. Logan and Larry Short, *Mobilizing for Compassion* (Grand Rapids: Fleming H. Revell, 1994).

Chapter 10

1. "The Numbers News," *American Demographics*, May 1994, n. p.

Chapter 11

1. George R. Walther, "Your Secret Opportunity," in *SUCCESS*, May 1992, 12.

Chapter 12

1. Reported in *Illustration Digest*, June–August 1993, 14.

Chapter 13

1. See Neil Anderson, *Setting Your Church Free* (Ventura: Regal Books, 1994).

2. For a live presentation of the principles found in this book, call Dr. Gary L. McIntosh at (909) 882-5386 or write him at The Church Growth Network, 3630 Camellia Dr., San Bernardino, CA 92404.